This book is a brilliant, personal and ultimately hopeful journey through grief and beyond. While dealing with death, it is also about the loss, disappointment and suffering we all experience. Alain wrestles with the mystery of woundedness and the painful journey of being transformed by the love of God through suffering. If you don't want grief to define you forever, read this book.

PETER LYNAS
Northern Ireland Director, Evangelical Alliance

Luminous Dark is, quite simply, one of the most powerful books I have ever read. I couldn't put it down. This is a book to be read by all who have experienced suffering and grief – and all who will do so in the future. It brings together the experience of a young man who faces the sudden death of his 23-year-old wife; it is illustrated by his poetic and honest journaling; and it is deeply rooted in theology and modern culture.

If you are anything like me, you will probably weep your way through it. Whatever else, don't miss it! A beautifully written Christian book which should become a classic.

THE RT REVD HAROLD C MILLER
Church of Ireland Bishop of the Diocese of Down & Dromore

I had the painful privilege of walking with Alain through the valley of the shadow of death. It was hard watching him stare down his grief and vulnerably wrestle with God. As I read *Luminous Dark* I am thankful that he has told us what he saw down that tough dark road. This is a theologically thoughtful and pastorally powerful resource for us all – a sweet song of catharsis from a shattered soul.

STEVE STOCKMAN
Minister of Fitzroy Presbyterian Church, Belfast;
Author of Walk on: The Spiritual Journey of U2

Through opening up his story, Alain opens up how we see God himself. There is no gloss painted over pain but there is a beautiful melody building throughout. A painfully raw read at times, yet full of honest hope. Having now read it once I want to go back and read it again slowly, because this is a story that shines so much light on God; I need to listen again.

HELEN WARNOCK

D0924057

Death, especially the death of a loved one, raises hard questions that touch on the very meaning of life. Alain faces these questions with honesty and realism. He not only describes the pain that lies in death's shadow but also how he encountered the Lord as his shepherd in helping him navigate the consequences of the loss of his beloved wife, Lindsay. Alain's book will help restore faith and confidence in God and bring light into dark places. I thoroughly recommend it.

JOHN LENNOX
Christian Apologist, Emeritus Professor of Mathematics
at the University of Oxford, and Lindsay's uncle

This raw and unflinching book urges those who love God, but who feel only confused betrayal in the face of loss, to press on into the Father's heart of love.

As we share with Alain the transformative experience of bereavement, he takes us on a journey through a valley of silent darkness to reach a place of unexpected revelation and paradoxical joy.

This book can also help our churches to discover a new and much-needed insight into grief and loss. It offers an interpretation and a vocabulary to reach those who are hurting, and promises the potential of God's rich and generous blessing on those who have been bereaved.

JANE OUNDJIAN
Founder of 'The Bereavement Journey' course, Holy Trinity, Brompton

Luminous Dark is an exceptional, inspiring, deeply courageous, and moving book. It is a meditation and spiritual response to the question 'What will you do with your pain?' In his book, Alain encourages us to embrace the pain of loss and offers one of the most sensitive and comprehensive books on the theology of grief in our time.

ANDREA WIGGLESWORTH, MSc
Counsellor, Psychotherapist and Life Coach

LUMI NOUS

DARK

LUMI NOUS

ALAIN
EMERSON

DARK

Muddy
Pearl

First published in 2017 by
Muddy Pearl, Edinburgh, Scotland.
www.muddypearl.com
books@muddypearl.com

© Alain Emerson 2017
Alain Emerson has asserted his right under the Copyright, Designs and Patents Act,
1988 to be identified as the author of this work.

'Girl on the edge of the photograph' and 'Caught between the mystery'
© Steve Stockman 2017, used with permission.

All rights reserved. No part of this publication may be reproduced or transmitted in
any form or by any means, electronic or mechanical, including photocopy, recording, or
information storage retrieval system, without permission in writing from the publisher. The
only exception is brief quotations in printed reviews of articles.

Unless otherwise indicated, Scripture quotations are taken from the ESV® Bible (The Holy
Bible, English Standard Version®), copyright © 2001 by Crossway, a publishing ministry of
Good News Publishers. Used by permission. All rights reserved.

Scripture quotations marked NIV taken from the Holy Bible, New International Version
Anglicized Copyright © 1979, 1984, 2011 Biblica. Used by permission of Hodder & Stoughton
Ltd, an Hachette UK Company. All rights reserved. NIV is a registered trademark of Biblica
UK trademark number 1448790.

Scripture quotations taken from The Message. Copyright © 1993, 1994, 1995, 1996, 2000,
2001, 2002 by Eugene H. Peterson. Used by permission of NavPress. All rights reserved.
Represented by Tyndale House Publishers, Inc.

Scripture quotations are taken from the Holy Bible, New Living Translation, copyright
©1996, 2004, 2007, 2013, 2015 by Tyndale House Foundation. Used by permission of Tyndale
House Publishers, Inc., Carol Stream, Illinois 60188. All rights reserved.

Scripture quotations marked NRSV are from the New Revised Standard Version Bible:
Anglicized Edition, copyright © 1989, 1995 National Council of the Churches of Christ in the
United States of America. Used by permission. All rights reserved worldwide.

Scripture quotations marked NKJV are taken from the New King James Version®. Copyright
© 1982 by Thomas Nelson. Used by permission. All rights reserved.

Scripture quotations from The Authorized (King James) Version. Rights in the Authorized
Version in the United Kingdom are vested in the Crown. Reproduced by permission of the
Crown's patentee, Cambridge University Press.

British Library Cataloguing in Publication Data
A catalogue record for this book is available from the British Library.

ISBN 978-1-910012-45-1

Cover design by Jeff Miller
Typeset in Minion by Waverley Typesetters, Warham, Norfolk
Printed in Great Britain by Bell & Bain Ltd, Glasgow

Girl on the edge of the photograph
Who always seemed so distracted
The gift of your mischievousness
Was what left you so unaffected.

Girl on the edge of the photograph
Who could have been centre screen
The beauty about her beauty
Was she knew what beauty means.

Girl on the edge of the photograph
A heart with peripheral vision
The strength of your contrariness
Touched the corners of this world's derision.

Girl on the edge of the photograph
Who you could so easily miss
But not by those who watched you bow
To give their soul a kiss.

For Arthur and Liz, Zoe, Sancha and Nik

'Having loved his own … he loved them to the end.'
John 13:1

ACKNOWLEDGEMENTS

This book took everything I had in me to write; I couldn't have done it without so many people. With heartfelt thanks to all of you:

To Stephanie and Richard Heald, and all at Muddy Pearl, for believing that this was a story worth telling and for going the extra mile to get it published: thank you so much.

To all those who proofread and provided feedback: Nina, John Mac, Peter, Big Gav, Mel, Julie – you helped me believe it was worth pushing through when I didn't think it was worth it.

To Pete Greig for inspiring leadership, friendship and the foreword.

To Andrea Wigglesworth for encouragement to write my grieving revelations, but more importantly for wise counsel and love throughout those days.

To Steve Stockman for encouragement and the gift of words when I didn't have my own.

To friends who have stood with me through the worst days of my life and cheered on this book: Rick and Ruth, Brian and Tracey, Adrian and Jenny, Stefan, Neil, Dixie, Lisa, Glenn, Dave and Laura, Grant and Lyns, Helen, Stephanie, Ken and Sonya, Mark and Claire, Tash, Dave Mull, Lenny, Lynn, Keith, Jimmy, Myles and Phyllis.

To the staff, fellow elders and members of Emmanuel Church – there are too many of you to mention but you are my closest comrades and my greatest heroes. I feel deeply humbled to help lead you especially because in the darkest of days you led me. Special mention to Robert and Joy and my beautiful friend Gayle, who walked a similar road with profound dignity.

To everyone who travelled and contributed to the work in Jandira, *Webale nyo:* the dream became a reality because of you.

To Pastor Richard and the good people of Jandira, *Mukwano Gwange!*

To Phil, my friend and pastor and truest companion through the Valley of the Shadow.

To my mum and dad, Grace and Ricky, Wendy and John, Norma and Stuart and our ever-expanding beautiful tribe: all of my love. You got me through and I will never forget.

To Arthur and Liz, Zoe and Richard, Sancha and James, Nik and Hazel: you continue to mean so much to me, and together we loved Lindsay in ways I couldn't even find words to describe in this book.

To Annie and Erin: thank you for giving Daddy time to write and for generally being awesome.

To Rach: thank you for time, lavish amounts of patience and for being my primary encourager in writing this book. More than this, thank you for making my world better than I could ever have imagined it could be!

CONTENTS

FOREWORD

'There are precious holy moments in the travail of a soul burning with pain.'

I'm sitting beside Alain Emerson in his car on a wet, winter night outside Belfast's famous Crown Liquor Saloon on Great Victoria Street. Rain is clattering on the roof. Bruce Springsteen is playing on the stereo. And Alain is showing me photographs of the beautiful Irish girl he married two years ago and buried just a few days before our meeting.

I know it was Springsteen because his classic rendition of 'When the Saints' takes me back there every time I hear it.

At first the photographs reveal a beautiful young woman, newly married, luminously alive. A flick of the wrist, another line of the song, and we are in Africa. Lindsay is surrounded by laughing kids and she is laughing too.

We are all travelling in the footsteps of those who've gone before,
and we'll all be reunited, on a new and sunlit shore.

Here she is again, the same beautiful girl, but now she is sitting incongruously in a wheel chair.

And when the sun refuses to shine,
Lord, how I want to be in that number, when the saints
go marching in.

One way or another, I suppose the song was meant to be.
She's losing her hair. She's lying on clinical sheets.

And some say that this world of trouble, is the only world we'll
ever see …

Here come the pictures I've been dreading. She is gaunt and pale, hooked up to a cat's cradle of wires and intravenous drips. Alain falls silent. The windscreen wipers sigh.

But I'm waiting for that morning, when the new world is revealed.

'And this,' he says eventually, holding up the last, most frail photograph, nearly thrusting it in my face, 'this is the most beautiful of them all.' I almost believe him. There is a rage about him. A rage and a holiness.

I heard 'The Saints Go Marching In' on almost every page of this book, often pausing at particular paragraphs to dry my eyes; the tears that failed me back in Belfast, all those years ago.

It matters a great deal that it was more than a decade ago. No one should share such pain in public when their wounds are still raw. Alain has wisely waited to tell his tale, healing slowly with the help of friends and family, Bruce Springsteen and the odd, inevitable pint of Guinness too. The wisdom of this memoir flows in part, I think, from the wholeness of its author. *'The reason I write this book,'* he says, *'is not to simply tell you my story but to humbly encourage those of you facing what seems like insurmountable grief and irreversible anguish to lean into the pain. You may feel like you have lost your life, but you don't have to lose your soul.'*

Alain has learned to 'lean into the pain' of his own tragedy for sure. There are no magic pills on offer, no neat algorithm awaiting the final page. Instead you will find brutal honesty disguised in the most beautiful prose. And yet somehow, having suffered more than most young men of his age, Alain Emerson has turned his own 'irreversible anguish' into a message of defiant, resilient hope. He has retained his soul. In fact, he has probably catalyzed more concerted, united intercession in Ireland than any other member of his generation, in spite of – or perhaps, because of – his own tragic experiences of unanswered prayer.

It's another night at another bar, a year or so after Lindsay's death, 'You know that wee bit where Jesus promises us life to the full?' he asks and I nod, noticing the wry smile on Alain's face, wondering what's coming next.

'Well, has it ever occurred to you,' he says, with his head on one side, 'that when Jesus said "life to the full" he must surely have meant a life like his own?'

This doesn't seem particularly controversial or profound. I nod again and sip my drink.

'Life to the full means a life full of joy and miracles, like Jesus, right?'

I try to smile encouragingly. Where is he going with this?

Alain looks me directly in the eyes. 'But wasn't the life of Christ marked by suffering as well as joy? Wouldn't a life like his also be full of struggles, disappointment and pain?'

Caught off guard, I put down my drink. How had I missed such an obvious and important insight all my life? How often had I preached on this particular promise, emphasizing only the fullness of joy that Jesus comes to bring, but never the pain.

I looked at Alain and realized, not for the first time, that his suffering had granted him wisdom and empathy well beyond his years. You'll find that his story effervesces with similar, simple, hard-won insights like these. I have absolutely no doubt, therefore, that it is destined to bring comfort to many who suffer their own great loss, and to help countless others find healing in the hurt and in the very darkest of nights the gentle light eternal.

> Oh Lord how I want to be in that number,
> When the saints go marching in.

PETE GREIG
24-7 Prayer International, Emmaus Rd, Guildford

INTRODUCTION: RUNNING IN THE DARK

These days I love running in the dark. On winter nights when the air is cold, I set off for a gentle gallop through the streets of my hometown village. Chasing the long shadows of the street lamps as the fog from my own breath dissolves on my perspiring face, I run over the motorway bridge, stealing away from the noise of the late-night commuting traffic, through the spookily serene railway crossing and eventually into the darkness of the countryside. The only thing lighting my path is the low glow of my phone, helping me navigate ankle-damaging potholes and providing a precautionary warning light for the occasional car venturing down these winding country roads. It is dark and still, dangerous and eerie, yet I am not scared.

I no longer fear the darkness.

Even though the night appears vacant, the darkness is filled with, dare I say it, 'presence'. This is the place where I do my best thinking these days. The night is flooded with mysterious luminosity. It is here my mind and soul are laid bare, the imposter is exposed and my true self revealed. And I rediscover how deeply known and loved I am.

It hasn't always been that way though.

Like most people I have lived my life scared of the dark, fear gripping hold of my senses on many occasions. From night-time walks as a child, up the creaking long corridor while the whole house was asleep, to wandering the ghostly back streets of townships in Soweto, searching for runaway street-kids as a gap-year volunteer. Darkness for me has been synonymous with fear, confusion and disorientation. It has both frightened and disconcerted me, sending shivers through my spine and causing my knees to buckle. As Barbara Brown Taylor describes:

> '"Darkness", is shorthand for anything that scares me – that I want no
> part of – either because I am sure that I do not have the resources to
> survive it or because I do not want to find out.'[1]

Yet something changed when I learned, or rather was forced, to stare
darkness in the eye, when I was summoned to front it up square in
the face. I discovered something liberating happens when we
acknowledge the genuine fear we are experiencing from the darkness
that surrounds us and yet *refuse* to let that fear have the last say. Further,
the fear is disarmed when we discover there is a light concealed within
that very darkness. When we apprehend a certain quality to darkness
which draws us further in, beyond what normal feeling or thoughts
can comprehend. This is a discovery that cannot simply be learned in
abstraction, only *encountered* as we choose to *enter* in.

What do I mean? Let me try to explain.

In 2007, when I experienced the great loss of my life, I found myself
for long days walking down dark trails of grief ending only in cul-de-
sacs. This was due in equal measure to my inability to process my pain,
and the incapacity and ignorance of the culture around me to accept
the reality of loss and grief.

As a means of catharsis I began to write, journal and then,
more publically, blog some of my thoughts online. Initially this
was motivated simply by the fact that many of my friends where
compassionately seeking to walk with me through dark and lonely
days and as it was too painful to leave the house, the blog allowed
me to thank them and inform their kind prayers for me. But I found
the heart ponderings I was posting on my blog were gaining a much
wider readership than my immediate friends and family. Hundreds of
people seemed to be following my story. I wasn't particularly happy or
sad about this. I just found it interesting and slightly embarrassing that
a story so broken and thoroughly depressing was capturing people's
attention. I was worried it came across as nihilistic and self-indulgent;
there were far worse things happening in the world around us at the
time, as there are now, but I was just trying to be true to what I was

---

[1] Barbara Brown Taylor, *Learning to Walk in the Dark*, Canterbury Press (2014).

experiencing. People commented kindly, telling me they were praying for me and thinking about me. But then, as I continued to unravel the nature of my dark days in this blog form of processing, the comments people were leaving started to become more personal and vulnerable, then private emails appeared in my inbox and eventually a trickle of new acquaintances began to visit. They came to share with me their own broken stories: parents who had watched children die, family members of suicide victims, spouses who had lost lovers, singles who had never found soul-mates, friends who were watching companions deal with cancer diagnosis, invalids dealing with long term physical disabilities. Some of these stories people shared with me were recent and the pain was acute, others were dealing with a deeper pain and vacancy in their lives that had lingered for many years. The common denominator: all of them familiar with darkness.

I became aware that, like me, people did not know how to grieve, no one had taught them how to wrestle with pain, how to stare darkness in the eye, how to discover the permission to laugh again. Bewilderingly they were talking to me about it, a disillusioned twenty-seven-year-old widower, who most nights, wasn't sure if he was going to make it to the morning. All I was doing was being honest – describing how I *really* felt and figuring out as I journeyed through how to articulate a language for my soul. Not settling for trivialized answers or religious hyperbole, I simply said what I felt. More, I was trying to *pray* what I was experiencing. I didn't know if that was ok or not but like trying to submerge a beach-ball under water, it became almost impossible for me to hold my emotions down. The longer and more forcefully I tried to hold them down the more violently they burst up through me again. And because so much of my life was shaped in church and my relationship with God, he seemed like the most obvious person to express it all to. It was simply too painful, both physically and emotionally to let the darkness and agony settle inside me.

Ten years on, those days still haunt me. For some of you this is your current reality. For others, even in this introduction your heart has already been painfully jabbed as you recall those days of dense darkness that have never fully worked their way through you. My deepest hope and humble prayer is that this book will become a type of soul companion. A resource wherein you will find language and liturgy that initially connects with the darkness in your heart, helping soothe the bleak loneliness which engulfs you in these days that often persist for many years. Then in time I hope you can trust me to help you believe there may be a certain luminosity laden in the darkness currently flooding your senses.

More generally, however, I hope this book can connect with all who read it, for, truthfully, the valley of the shadow of death, and the way of suffering, grief and loss, is a terrain we all must travel at some point in this life. Loss is woven into the fabric of life and the choice we all have to make is *how* we will travel through this valley when it is our turn to walk it: we *will* lose the one we loved most in life; we *will* do something we never thought we would do; the ideal we carried for years *will* get smashed up right in front of our face; we *will* enter the cloud of unknowing for a season where the heavens seem like brass. Love and loss, presence and absence, suffering and resurrection; these are not sets of opposites, rather they ebb and flow together in this current of life on earth. Darkness in this world is as real for most people as light, pain more common than wholeness, loneliness more felt than belonging. Unfortunately, our church environments have developed what Barbara Brown Taylor describes as a 'full solar spirituality'[2] which only absorbs and reflects 'the sunny side of faith'. As a result, we are forced to try and navigate the traumatic emotions of isolation, fear and anxiety. The days are dark, the nights are darker and we are left, often alone, to choose how we will respond.

My experience has taught me that most of us don't know what to do. Of course, there is no formula. Bravely we may try to fight and grapple our way through the bleakness shrouding our new normal. But this is a lonely road, and for understandable reasons we often escape down any road that promises even a glimmer of light for respite, rather than pursing the 'true light' which can only be discovered as we choose to completely *move through* that darkness. A 'sunny spirituality' is inadequate for such a journey. It does not possess the skills to operate in the dark.

---

[2] Barbara Brown Taylor, *Learning to Walk in the Dark.*

Surprisingly though, we are much better equipped to deal with the darkness than what we think. John O'Donohue, that beautiful modern day mystic, argued 'darkness in one of our closest companions'.[3] We are, believe it or not, innately familiar with darkness. Creation itself was formed out of darkness, each one of us was formed in the darkness of the womb and, more trivially, we all love the idea of keeping a secret! For the Christian, this train of thought deepens when we reflect on how God incarnate was acquainted with grief and sorrow, hanging for three hours in total darkness. He 'made his bed in Sheol', shrouded in darkness in a guarded Roman tomb. Imagine, the Light of the World embodied the darkness of the world and of every human heart. His light and presence concealed in a dead body in a dark tomb. Yet even when it seemed the lights had completely gone out the story hadn't finished. The Light would have the last word. The resurrection reminds us that ultimately this light shines *in* the darkness and the darkness cannot overcome it or comprehend it.

Not only are we image-bearers of the One who suffers loss with us, a non-forsaking companion for the dark days; we also have a forerunner who has moved through a mysterious and monumental intensity of darkness we cannot comprehend. In a sense God in Christ has lit up every dark place in our hearts with his Light because he has taken that darkness *into* himself and showered it with his glorious and victorious light. When we embrace the darkness wholeheartedly and pray it before his face, eventually an inextinguishable light will rise up within us as resurrection life.

The church fathers of the Christian tradition discovered this subversive truth hundreds of years ago, long before I did. Their writings and works helped me through my own journey and now serve as an inspiration for the title of this book – *Luminous Dark*. They had perceived through experience that true enlightenment for life and faith came through an embrace of the darkness and would go as far as to argue 'darkness is the cradle of growth'.

---

[3] John O'Donohue, *Eternal Echoes: Exploring Our Hunger to Belong*, Bantam, new edition (2 November 2000).

Gregory of Nyssa, one such example, described in his work *The Life of Moses* the way pilgrims could fearlessly approach the darkness for they had come to realize that it was through these seasons they could apprehend a deeper truth, attain a richer wisdom and encounter a place where mere understanding does not reach.

> Since Moses was alone, by having been stripped as it were of the people's fear, he boldly approached the very darkness itself and entered the invisible things where he was no longer seen by those watching. After he entered the inner sanctuary of the divine mystical doctrine, there, while not being seen, he was in company with the Invisible. He teaches, I think, by the things he did that the one who is going to associate intimately with God must go beyond all that is visible and – lifting up his own mind, as to a mountaintop, to the invisible and incomprehensible – believe that the divine is there where the understanding does not reach.[4]

Gregory of Nyssa and the wise sages of church history gave us a whole new level of understanding of the relationship between light and darkness in the Judeo-Christian faith. They released the wisdom and beauty contained in the first chapter of John's Gospel. 'The light shines *in* the darkness ...' The light shines in, not outside or into the darkness, but *in* the darkness. This light more than simply the natural light we see and experience, *inheres* the darkness and when it is illuminated we witness an infinitely more beautiful, translucent and transformational light that shatters the opaque circumstances of our lives.

Arguably no one said, or sang, this better that the Psalmist:

> If I say, 'Surely the darkness shall cover me,
> and the light about me be night,'
> even the darkness is not dark to you;
> the night is bright as the day,
> for darkness is as light with you.
>
> Psalm 139:11-12

---

[4] Gregory of Nyssa, *The Life of Moses*, HarperCollins (1 July 2008).

some advice and caveats for the reader

The first few chapters of the book during the great loss of my life and the subsequent days of survival. They are intense. This may be too much for some – I understand. This book may not be for you or may be for another time. But I wanted to really engage with people who *are* experiencing such stark hopelessness and what seems like unrelenting waves of traumatic grief. I felt strongly exercised to validate the extreme loneliness that is an all-consuming reality in such tragic days. We dare not trivialize or ignore. Firstly, because there is a holy power, a kind of sacred pathos released in the vulnerability of powerlessness that acknowledges the pain our fellow humanity has endured. Secondly in fully validating this pain there is something to discover, a treasure to mine if we can get to the bottom of the darkness.

Chapter three is a watershed moment. After describing my own tragic brokenness of belonging, I invite the reader to come on the journey through the luminous darkness, leaning into the pain, in the hope of transformation. The ensuing chapters (chapter four onwards) are therefore my attempt to do such describing the key stages of my luminous darkness.

The danger with highlighting one particular story in a book is that it can invalidate other people's stories. Please don't allow this to be the case but rather come with me on this journey carrying the personal disappointments and questions of your story with you for there is a sacredness to each one of our lives beyond which we can fully grasp. My hope for this book is that whatever chapter you find yourself in, in your own story of life, you will find threads of truth in my journey that will connect yours.

I've tried to be as true to myself as I can be. As you will have guessed already, I am a Christian and have been nurtured in that faith tradition all my life. My thoughts and worldviews are therefore shaped from an understanding of what it means to be a disciple of Jesus Christ. The reconstruction of my life in light of my loss provokes a challenge to the predisposed way many evangelical Christians understand some of our fundamental thinking. I hope you can hear my heart in this, as I reconstructed a completely shattered Biblical worldview. Equally if you are not a Christian, or from a different tradition of faith, I hope you will not find this disengaging. Rather I would encourage you to stay curious with me as I try to genuinely wrestle myself into a reoriented faith space.

While this book focuses more internally on the wrestlings and wranglings of a fragile soul coming to terms with acute pain and loss I want to acknowledge the other practical implications associated with such difficult days. Many people, in addition to the agony of soul they have experienced, have complex day-to-day concerns to cope with such as finances, disabilities, marriage tensions and intense parenting stresses. It is beyond the purposes of this book to deal with these specifically but it would be insincere not to acknowledge how intrinsic these issues can be in the journey towards wholeness.

With all this said, let me begin by telling you my story.

CHAPTER ONE

THE LOSS

We all lose things in life. Every day. The car keys, the TV remote, or, worst of all, the mobile phone. Typically, this happens at the most inconvenient times – when we are already late for work, when the match is about to start, when we urgently need to make a phone call. Tensions escalate, tempers fray, we summon everyone within range to join the emergency search party. Eventually, the calmest person in the room finds the lost item, hands it back to us and there is a sense of relief. Life is ok again.

Sometimes we lose things that we never get back in this life. This is the worst kind of loss – the loss of a dream, the loss of innocence, the loss of someone we love. Things we had hoped to keep forever just slip away, and are gone. It may be sudden – a shocking blow that leaves us bewildered and broken. Or it may be that loss comes gradually, gnawing away at our souls, until one day we have to accept the brutal reality that our hope, our treasure, is gone. We are left to work out how to grieve our way through a future we had never planned. Our dreams are shattered, our ideals smashed, our hopes crushed. Our souls bleed pain and sorrow; our minds are tormented in confusion and doubt. This is where I found myself at the tender age of twenty-seven.

LINDSAY ANDERSON

The 8th June 2005 was the best day of my life. Lindsay Jane Anderson had just become Mrs Emerson. I felt like a king!

I had met Lindsay about four years before. It was pre-church worship practice when she arrived early with her dad, Arthur, and focusing on the worship became suddenly very difficult. She was strikingly attractive, her movements carried mystery, and she had a natural confidence that made my insides do somersaults. I had never laid eyes on her before, never spoken to her, and yet it felt like I already knew her. As it turned out, my dad knew Arthur from way back, which I chose to believe was the providence of the Almighty, and the perfect opportunity to introduce ourselves. I played it as cool as I could, trying to match her much more natural poise. After a five-minute chat on the steps of the church that Sunday morning, I would think about Lindsay Jane Anderson every single day for the next six years.

At that time there was a bit of a buzz around the youth church that I was helping to lead – there was a sense of excitement, a lot of energy, people were encountering God and we looked forward to meeting together on Friday nights, and on Sundays. Lindsay was very much at the centre, with her natural confidence, but the thing I admired most was she was also always picking people up from around the edges.

After a year of occasional conversations and brief flirtations we finally had 'the chat'. I plucked up the courage to ask her: 'Would you kinda like, sorta like, maybe like, no worries if you don't wanna like, go out with me?' She said: 'Sure, let's see how it goes'. I was head over heels. Two years later, I proposed to her in front of all our closest friends. She said yes. I had found my soulmate and it was better than I ever imagined it could be.

Life with Lindsay was an adventure. She never seemed particularly conscious of her looks, but was often asked by hairstylists to be a model – which meant she got her hair cut for free, but also that she would turn up with all sorts of weird and wonderful hairstyles. I remember one Sunday, I had been asked to speak at a fairly traditional church in County Down. I came to pick her up, she got in the car with a nonchalant 'hiya' as if everything was normal. I did a double take, 'Holy smoke that's bright!' Her hair was shocking crimson. I stopped worrying about my talk and began to worry what the congregation would make of us. I needn't have – she had soon completely won them over. She had a way of connecting with people of all ages, a maturity way beyond her years.

Eighteen months later we were married. We were full of youthful idealism about the future and how we would serve God together. Inspired by Jesus' description of his Spirit being like the wind we vowed to live obediently and adventurously blown by the Spirit of God wherever he would have us go.

We bought an apartment with one room downstairs and a bedroom upstairs. It was simple and small, yet the setting for a magical time, the start of our married life together. What we lacked in money and space we made up for in fun and creativity. Content in our mutual determination never to be defined by what we might own or acquire, we treated our home as a base from which to plan and anticipate the adventures that lay ahead.

AUNTIE JILL

One Wednesday night, about nine months into our marriage, Lindsay and I had just returned home from a night out when I received the most terrible phone call of my life. My auntie Jill had suddenly died. She had come home from a women's meeting in church, climbed into bed beside her husband and, as he asked her how the meeting had gone, literally died in his arms. Jill Emerson was my fun-loving, dream-catcher of an auntie who, alongside my uncle Phil, had pioneered and planted our church, Emmanuel, Lurgan. At the age of 48 and with no previous health problems, she was suddenly gone.

Phil and Jill were the closest of family and dearest of friends. Their four children matched up easily with my three sisters and me at similar ages, and we spent a good part of our lives together. Meals out, sleepovers, cinema trips and joint holidays had given us a legacy of beautiful memories.

Phil and Jill. The lilting rhyme of their names mirrored the deep affection they had for one another and the inseparable nature of their married life. They were the most reluctant, down-to-earth leaders you could find, who made themselves available to God to serve the most broken of our local community. Their attitude of simple obedience has affected thousands of lives. The first ten years of our church family's life was a wild and exhilarating faith adventure. From a handful of people meeting in their home and spending most of their time around their table, eating and sharing life together, the church had grown to over 200, from all sorts of backgrounds. Yet they held to the same strong family values the church had been established on. When she died so unexpectedly, the impact on her immediate family, and the wider church family, was colossal.

When I received the call, I raced to the house. I will never forget Phil coming down the stairs from the bedroom where his wife's body lay lifeless, his face hidden in his hands, utterly broken. I couldn't believe what was happening. I had chatted with her, laughed with her, worked alongside her that very day.

Now she was dead.

My uncle Phil was one of my closest friends – we spent most days together dreaming and shaping the church we had given our lives to. Over the next couple of days, I watched him, the man who had been an inspiration to me for years, fall into a black hole of unimaginable pain. I was heartbroken at losing my wonderful auntie, who had left a lasting impression on my life. Yet it was the picture of Phil, my strong-spirited uncle and inspirational leader, reduced to a grieving and despairing child, that I will never forget. As the weeks unfolded I felt compassion well up inside me and a desire to be with him whenever I could. We walked together almost every day. 'Walking helps', Phil would say resting his hand delicately on his chest. 'If you sit down it hurts too much.' After a walk in the park we would go back to his house, I would make a cup of tea and sit at the table, while Phil just kept walking – round and round, lap after lap of the carpet in his kitchen. Sometimes he would say nothing, other times he would talk about his loss, his fears for the future, his concern for his four grown-up children who were coming to terms with losing their mother. This was the closest I had been to death and it was haunting to watch.

For me it was a stretching time. Helping to lead the church through this crisis wasn't a challenge I was expecting during my first year of marriage, but I was determined to respond well. Lindsay and

I sought to emulate the marriage of Phil and Jill. In these terrible circumstances we resolved to live out the vows we had committed to each other a year earlier — to be blown by the wind of God, wherever he wanted to take us. We stepped in to help in leadership, going to Albania to support a sister church six weeks after auntie Jill died, spending time training up their leaders; and then that summer we were off again to Uganda to lead a mission trip and pioneer new work there. The timing was not ideal, as I was reluctant to leave Phil, but with his blessing Lindsay and I set off, knowing that as we went we were fulfilling a shared dream.

AFRICA

Africa was our favourite continent: the history, people and culture had already gotten firmly under our skin even before we were engaged. During her gap year, Lindsay had spent two months in South Africa with Christian Aid and, later, another five weeks in Burkina Faso with Tearfund. She was deeply impacted by her experiences in Africa and her time there matured her passion for social justice in ways, it seemed, that would start to determine the direction of her life.

I, too, had fallen for Africa. At the age of nineteen I had spent a year in South Africa, working with street kids in a shelter on the outskirts of Johannesburg. Africa was where I found myself, and, more importantly, found God. I fell in love with this enchanting part of the world. Subsequent trips led me back to South Africa, Ghana and Uganda, all granting the most life-giving experiences and unforgettable memories. When we knew we would spend the rest of our lives together, it seemed only a matter of time before we would board a plane to Africa together.

On this trip we spent a month in Uganda, leading a team of forty people from our church to help with building projects for a local primary school in a remote village called Jandira. There we met Pastor Richard, and connected deeply and profoundly with him and the work he had committed his life to. We came back changed, and dreaming of committing to this work longer term, perhaps one day helping to build a much-needed secondary school for the community.

THE LOSS

After we returned from Uganda, Lindsay was troubled by headaches. She was completing her International Studies degree but was struggling with pain and tiredness. After many appointments and prescriptions, Lindsay underwent a precautionary CT scan. As we were waiting for the results a consultant approached us and kindly asked us to come into his office. It was here that we heard the news. Lindsay had a 'growth' in her brain. Growth? I later learned that the term 'growth' is oncologists' code for brain tumour in the initial stage of breaking the news. I could feel my insides going numb. A routine hospital check-up on a lousy Monday afternoon had been interrupted by the soul-destroying news that would change our world. A sense of despair pervaded my being, and fear was crawling all over my skin. As we walked back through the hospital, a parallel world opened before me, making everything and everyone feel further away, and a surreal emptiness invaded my insides. I helped Lindsay into the car and for a moment I couldn't get in beside her. I called my dad in the car park and as he answered I began to weep. I had never been so scared.

We were asked to return to the hospital that night, the locus of our lives for the coming months. Four days later Lindsay was wheeled into theatre to have brain surgery. As I watched her disappear through the swinging hospital doors, my stomach began to churn with apprehension. I walked to the canteen to begin the long wait and in a kind of a role reversal, just six months after auntie Jill had died, Phil was there, waiting to sit through the long and tortuous hours with me.

Initially the prognosis was positive. Lindsay came through the operation well, and we were told it was a success – they had managed to remove 95% of the tumour. Critically, however, it was too deep to remove all of it without damaging her other cognitive faculties. This was a grade 3 tumour, meaning there was a strong likelihood it could return. However, the surgeon told us he was pleased with the operation and that we should 'get on with living our lives and fulfilling our dreams'. He encouraged us to travel and have kids, and Lindsay and I, along with our incredibly supportive friends and families, dared to hope and believe that the tumour would shrink and Lindsay would be completely healed.

Within a month Lindsay looked as good as she always did and within two months her surgeon asked her to take part in an open lecture with other brain surgeons as a case study of a successful operation.

As we approached Christmas 2006, our initial hopes were dashed when Lindsay experienced two seizures in the space of a week. This prompted a second round of brain surgery, followed by six weeks of chemotherapy and radiotherapy. Slowly but surely Lindsay grew weaker. Clumps of hair started to fall out, her legs started to weaken and by March 2007 her speech started to go. At 27 years of age I found myself taking my wife for walks in a wheelchair, spoon-feeding her meals and taking her to the bathroom. I was aided by Lindsay's wonderful family and my own. Together we journeyed through Lindsay's sickness in love, carrying with us a tangible sense of peace. We tended to her needs and loved her with everything we had within us. Eventually Lindsay lost the ability to do anything for herself, but in spite of this she maintained the most profound sense of courage and dignity I have ever witnessed.

Carried by the prayers and faith of our church community and many others we continued to hope for Lindsay's recovery. Our family, friends and local church, who were still in a place of grief after the loss of Jill, rallied and prayed for Lindsay's life every night for many weeks. They gave everything they could. Their prayers and mine didn't seem to have an effect on Lindsay physically, but they did something profound in my soul. I am convinced these prayers galvanized a resolve and strength of covenantal love. In the midst of my brokenness I could feel my heart enlarging with an intensity of love and compassion for Lindsay that I never imagined was possible to feel for someone.

The extremes of emotion I was experiencing were beyond anything I had ever known, yet they were genuine. It seemed that the less beautiful she became outwardly the more her *real beauty* captivated my heart. I remember thinking I was too superficial to experience this depth and purity of love. Even though Lindsay couldn't physically offer me any of her love in those days I was deeply aware of all the ways she perfected and completed me. I couldn't escape the anguish of seeing my stunning wife reduced almost to a vegetative state, yet there was a beautiful, profound peace as I looked into her eyes. I had discovered a boundless reservoir of love deep within me for her.

Lindsay's speech deteriorated to the point where she could not string any words together, but she was able to gently sing. Often as I sat at her bedside stroking her hand or face she would slowly sing one line to me repeatedly – the chorus to Blur's hit single 'Tender'. It was the sweetest lullaby:

> Oh my baby, oh my baby, all right, all right.[1]

During her sickness she would sing often to me and when she lost the ability to sing, I followed her lead and sang it back to her.

The room Lindsay lay in as we cared for her was charged with a gentle but powerful peace. She loved to meditate on a line of scripture: 'he makes me to lie down in green pastures'. She would often gesture to me to read this to her. On one occasion one of the community nurses left her bedroom in tears. Visibly moved, she asked me earnestly: 'What's in there?' The nurse had been touched by the presence of God tenderly gracing Lindsay's room. The sick room had become a 'thin place', a sanctuary, a kind of prayer room – as one by one her brother and sisters, mum and dad, and close friends would keep watch, reading scripture, praying gentle prayers, singing lullabies.

But she wasn't getting better.

On our final check-up in hospital, after the chemotherapy and radiotherapy had been completed, the oncologist and head nurse asked me to meet them for a few moments alone. They had just assessed

---

[1] Blur, 'Tender'.

Lindsay's failing speech and continued debilitation. Mrs Harney, the oncologist, said to me: 'Alain, we need you to know Lindsay is really sick'. Looking back now it was the nicest possible way they could say: 'We don't think she is going to make it'. I thanked them for their loving concern and reminded them that we knew God was with us and we were still praying for a miracle. But it was in that moment and on that journey home from the hospital that the calm I had been carrying for the previous weeks began to crack. I didn't know what to do other than fast and pray. For thirteen days I touched no food and cried out to God with everything, every part of my being.

One morning during this fast I sat at Lindsay's bedside and became embroiled in the fiercest, most intense and heart-wrenching tug-of-war with God. There was nothing more I could do. If there is such a thing as a spiritual checklist for times like this (I don't believe there is) then I had ticked every box. I had done everything I could before God, yet she was slowly slipping away from me. I told God that I wasn't finished fighting, that I wasn't giving up, and pleaded with him not to take her. Yet somehow, someway, I knew I needed to recognize his overarching plan and sovereign will. My only comfort in this titanic tussle was the conviction that, as her Heavenly Father, he loved her more than I did. Deep down I knew this was true but I had to muster up every ounce of faith left in me to *choose* to believe it. I quickly squared with God that even though he might love her more than I did, and I had to trust him with this, it was no reason to take her from me. I told God that if I had to compete with him for the depth of love he had for Lindsay I was running him pretty close.

I had always found that writing a journal was helpful, and in this intense season of my life opportunities to pour out my heart and head on paper kept me sane. That terrible holy morning, I wrote my own Gethsemane prayer in my journal:

Father, this is ripping my heart apart. This is almost unbearable. I know your grace is and will be sufficient but I am pleading with you to speak the word, Lord ... Just looking at her surely is enough for you to speak the word, to breathe that breath, God? I know you love her more than I do. I know and will believe you do … I feel I have entered into something of the torment of that moment when Jesus uttered 'not my will but thine be done'. But unlike Jesus I am unsure of what happens next and so I will fight on for her life.

DEATH

A week later, on Sunday 22nd April 2007, 6.30am, I awoke in the bed beside Lins and watched her gasp for breath. I panicked as the period in between breaths became longer and longer. How could I help her? How could I help her breathe more normally? There was nothing I could do. When the nurse arrived, she examined Lindsay's body and turned to us with a sympathetic slow shake of the head. I will never forget the look on her face.

It was over and she was gone. She was only 23.

Lindsay was dead.

I clung to Lindsay's body, still warm, and wailed from my innermost depths.

She was gone and I still had so much love left to give her.

I had not imagined Lindsay would die. I just never thought it would happen. I wasn't prepared for it at all. I was engulfed with anguish and pain. Utter disbelief gave way to a daunting, haunting realization that she wasn't coming back. Ever. The harsh cruelty and absolute finality of her death clashed violently with every fibre of my being.

Well-wishers came to pay their respects and to mourn with me. I am indebted to so many of them, for I am not sure I could have got through without them.

The odd person lovingly whispered to me in their embrace: 'At least you know where she is now'. Firstly, when coming alongside someone who is grieving, never start a sentence with 'at least'; secondly, it is hard to find consolation in this well-intentioned statement. In pent up frustration I wanted to howl back. 'No, I only know where she is NOT. She is NOT beside me in bed, she is NOT on the other end of the phone, she is NOT sitting beside me, she is NOT holding my hand'.

The assurance of Lindsay's security in heaven didn't soothe my mind the way I thought it should, such was the all-encompassing presence of her absence. I knew it was the great hope that I needed to cling to, but it just felt distant and abstract in those early days.

Our church family were warriors of love in these days as they rallied to pray for us, visit us, cook for us and weep with us. They had lost another leader, another friend and they still found a way to give Phil and me space to grieve yet also to grieve themselves. We tried our best to lead them through it, but they carried us and each other – they came together with one another in church, in their homes and in coffee shops – bearing one another's burdens, drying one another's tears, pulling each other through.

On the Friday night after Lindsay died – when they would have been meeting together and worshipping God together, the young people of Emmanuel came. There were around fifty or sixty of them – they parked a little way up the road from the house, gathered outside the front window for a moment, and lit candles. For a while they stood and prayed, and then in single file they walked around the house, with their candles, praying. Then they quietly went off to their cars and left. It was the perfect gesture of prayer, sympathy and respect, giving me space I needed but letting me know they were with me, praying.

Tuesday brought the funeral. I had stood at the front of our church less than two years before acknowledging and declaring my love to Lindsay in front of 200 people. Now I was standing at the same place in the same church in front of 1,000 people staring with disbelief at her coffin. How did I get here? I had cried so many tears that by the time of the funeral it felt like I had nothing left. Instead I felt empty and numb, stumbling around drunk in my own grief.

Phil, who had endured the funeral of his own wife so recently, was now conducting the funeral for mine. My close friend and gifted writer, Steve Stockman, mentor to both Lindsay and me during our days at university, helped articulate the collective sense of injustice, confusion and grief amongst those gathered to mourn Lindsay's death.

Caught between the mystery

We come with faith
But the theology don't rhyme
We come with hope
But we are all out of time
We come with reason to believe
But reason isn't what it was
We come with words that fail us

But Jesus never does
Faces stained with the love we cherished
Our hearts broken into a million pieces
It's the hardest thing you can ever do
Give your love into the arms of Jesus
And I know today Lindsay is singing
But it don't make this anymore right
To be caught between the mystery of darkness
And the mystery of God's good light.

After the graveside service, hundreds of people came back to the church to offer their love, comfort and support. Each one represented a different aspect of Lindsay's life and our lives together. My tears flowed in one wave of emotion after another. She was not just my wife, but a daughter, a sister, a niece, a cousin, an influencer, an encourager, a team member, a friend.

After the funeral we all went back to Lindsay's parents' house. Lindsay's dad poured me a glass of red wine to help me settle. While I sipped it I observed how Lindsay's family and mine were as united in our grief as we had been in our love for her during her sickness. It was very special, but then the realisation hit me — the one who had tied our families together was gone. The reason I had come to love her mother and father, her brother and sisters as my own, was gone. Would our relationship change? In the back of my mind a fear was developing: *everything* would change. Everything.

ALONE

Exhausted and emotionally spent, I fell into bed, a single bed. Though we hadn't shared a bed for weeks during Lindsay's sickness she was still beside me; her bodily presence within touching distance. Getting into bed on my own was a cruel reality and it carried with it a profound loneliness. I took her journal to bed with me that night, carefully reading the personal things she had written about me, her sickness and her conversations with God. I read the text messages she had sent me over the previous months that I had made sure were saved in my phone. These words were all I had left of her. As I poured over them, I longed for an apparition of her, something to help me 'feel' her close. If I could I would have gathered up all her words in her journal and swallowed them just to know that she was still part of me, still inside me. Her words brought a semblance of her to me and led me to instinctively reach out for her hand, but it wasn't there.

I was on my own.

Except I wasn't on my own.

> If I make my bed in Sheol, you are there!
>
> Psalm 139:8

I couldn't feel God and there was nothing I wanted to say to him at this moment, but instinctively, even in my own living hell, I knew he was there. God was there. I believed enough in what I had preached for years to know he was there, silent and watching. I didn't know what to say to him but it felt like I needed to say something. And so I prayed, or at least I wrote my thoughts to God, as an attempt to pray. I was desperately confused that my Father had let this happen. I had known him as my Father for most of my life and so, more out of habit than desire, I still addressed him as Father and poured out these words on a page.

Father, today I buried my beautiful Lins ... I am now a broken man. I do not want to go on without her. I miss her too much. I miss her hand touching mine, and my feet rubbing hers. She was 'my' Lins ... It hurts like hell. I cannot understand why you took her. I cannot and will not forget ... What will I do? Where will I go? Jesus help me. Help me to let you into my pain. Father, I love you but I can't see you or feel like I can hold you. Help me to trust you are holding me.

CHAPTER TWO

SURVIVAL

Save me, O God!
For the waters have come up to my neck.
I sink in deep mire,
where there is no foothold;
I have come into deep waters,
and the flood sweeps over me.

Psalm 69:1–2

On one of my trips to Africa I went whitewater rafting on the River Nile – without question the scariest, most exhilarating experience of my life. When we capsized in the maelstrom of a grade 5 rapid I thought my life was over. The river surged with such velocity and violence that, even mustering all my strength to try to ride the waves, I was powerless. It was like being dropped into a giant washing machine and pummeled, mercilessly, relentlessly from side to side. I was completely helpless, unable to summon any rational thought about escape or survival and was reduced to simply closing my eyes in hope that I might surface for air. I was probably submerged for only seven or eight seconds but it felt like an eternity. Only when I resurfaced did the realization dawn that I was still alive and was going to see my family again. A period of calm rowing on stretches of still water gave me time to overcome the disorientation and allowed my heartbeat to regain a degree of regularity. But it wasn't long before I heard, somewhere in the distance, a loud and intimidating rumble. I couldn't yet see it, but another giant rapid was moving closer, threatening to take me under all over again.

This is the best metaphor I can think of for traumatic and acute grief. Those who have been shipwrecked by grief will know what I mean. Like the intensity of the Nile's overpowering rapids, the early days of acute grief can be summed up in one word: SURVIVAL!

SURVIVAL

The relentless pounding and thrashing of waves of grief in the early days was disorientating and debilitating. I felt my body failing and my mind cracking. The point of reference in my life had gone, and so navigating the future – which at this point meant the next couple of hours – felt pointless and doomed to failure. C.S. Lewis's personal experience of grief caused him to observe: '… in grief nothing "stays put". One keeps on emerging from a phase, but it always recurs. Round and round. Everything repeats.'[1]

It wasn't a matter of simply moving through the phases of grief one after another, in a straight line. It was just being ready to face the unpredictability of whatever the next day threw at you – disappointment, denial, anger, acceptance – and in no particular order. Anne Lamott, in the days after her close friend died, experienced the same unpredictable power of grief:

> Grief, as I read somewhere once, is a lazy Susan. One day it is heavy and underwater, and the next day it spins and stops at loud and rageful, and the next day at wounded keening, and the next day numbness, silence.[2]

In those early days I was, quite simply, unable to control my grief – it controlled me. There are seasons of life we go through when this will be our experience. Our ache is so all-encompassing, our loss so severe, our emptiness so overwhelming that all we can do is ride out the

---

[1] C.S. Lewis, *A Grief Observed*, HarperCollins (2001).
[2] Anne Lamott, *Travelling Mercies: Some Thoughts on Faith*, Thorndike (1999).

waves that come crashing towards us. Grief towered over me like an angry giant threatening to crush me into the ground. I remember the advice Phil gave me. He encouraged me to split the day up into three – morning, afternoon and evening, 'Try to make it through the morning, Al, then focus on the afternoon and finally try to make it to bedtime when at least another day will be over.'

The depressingly basic goal of each day was simply to get to the end of it. Inevitably though, any bloody-minded resolve I could gather within myself would be battered by another juggernaut of grief. During these onslaughts my whole being would be overcome by darkness and flooded with emotion. It felt like I was being sucked into a dark and frightful abyss. I spent hours sitting at Lindsay's grave, gazing at photographs of her and talking about her to my family and closest friends, all the while clutching tightly to her wedding ring, which I had tied to a piece of string around my wrist. I clung to anything that would trigger a memory or make her presence seem a little more tangible; easing the pain for a nanosecond, until reality came hurtling towards me again.

The aim of each new day was just to make it through that day, and then the next one and then the next one. If you have been there you know what I mean. It is the darkest of dark hours and the only purpose in life is survival. To describe the intensity of the battle in these 'survival days', I think of soldiers trapped as the enemy closes in, or prisoners of war undergoing the horrors of isolation and torture. I came to know what it feels like to live your days realizing that you have nothing to live for other than to merely stay alive. You simply can't get any perspective. As C.S. Lewis described it: 'You can't see anything properly while your eyes are blurred with tears.'[3]

During these days we do what we need to do to get through – walking, talking, crying, writing, reading – whatever works. The cruel and ironic contradiction of this is that while any energy you can muster is concentrated on surviving, *most of your being doesn't really want to survive*. Life itself becomes meaningless.

---

[3] C.S. Lewis, *A Grief Observed*.

WHERE DOES THE LOVE GO NOW?

One disturbing question haunted me more than others in these days, positioning itself as a roadblock to progress. The question was framed in the beautifully haunting lyric from the band Lies Damned Lies: 'Where does the love go now?'[4] This question captured my deep agony and confusion, for I was aware there remained within me a vast reservoir of love in my heart for Lindsay. *But where does the love go now?* I stumbled around in my grief asking this question in frustration to my family and closest friends, *'Where does the love go now, Mum?' 'Dad, what do I do with all this love I have in my heart for Lins?' 'Someone please give me an answer!'*

The tenderness I felt for Lindsay was still swelling inside and threatening to overflow the dams of my heart. I wanted to care for her, protect her, look after her. But *where does the love go now?* The months preceding her death had been so intense yet so full of love, a love with a purity that was outside of this world. It was a love beyond words, literally, as she couldn't speak anymore. When we looked into one another's eyes something profound took place. It was deeply wounded but it was desperately wonderful. The poet Robert Burns in his poem, *Ae Fond Kiss And Then We Sever*, articulated it from his own experience of loss:

> Had we never lov'd sae kindly,
> Had we never lov'd sae blindly!
> Never met – or never parted,
> We had ne'er been broken-hearted.[5]

Despite the pain of watching Lindsay suffer and my frustration of not being able to 'fix it' for her, we touched heaven. We loved like heaven

---

[4] Lies Damned Lies, 'Where does the love go now?'
[5] Robert Burns, *Ae Fond Kiss And Then We Sever*.

loves. It was this love that was still pulsing through my being for her after she had gone and so the question *where does the love go now?* tortured me for days. I was living my own personal hell. Elder Zosima, in the epic *Brothers Karamazov*, describes hauntingly what my new understanding (and taste) of hell had become: 'I ask myself: "What is hell?" And I answer thus: "Hell is the suffering of being no longer able to love."'[6]

Love had wrung my heart out and left it out to dry. I had loved her from a place deep within me and now there was an inconsolable ache in that same place. The power of that love had broken the crust of my soul and chiseled its way agonizingly into the depths of my being. Now, in the very centre of me, I was exposed, and over the days and weeks ahead the pain continued to percolate through me. My broken prayers continued.

> This is the most desolate place. No one who has not been there could ever understand. It is like being punched in the stomach every minute of the day. C.S. Lewis describes it like the feeling of fear … The fluttering of the stomach, the restlessness, the continual swallowing. It feels like you are drowning and all your energy is being put into trying to find air for the next breath. It seems there is an invisible blanket that exists between me and the world. I am oblivious to everything around me. It feels like the world has been robbed of its most beautiful gift and yet the irony is that the world keeps going on as normal. Every road my thoughts take at the minute have lost their target – Lindsay – my thoughts keep running into a dead end and the pain of that is unbearable. The last two nights, I have genuinely felt like I may not make it to the morning and worse than that I am not sure I have even wanted to. I know there is a light somewhere – I am choosing to believe there is – but at the minute I cannot see it.

---

[6] Fyodor Dostoevsky, *The Brothers Karamazov*, Vintage Classics (16 January 1992).

WHERE DOES YOUR LOVE GO?

Maybe you are carrying a similar sense of loss or lack or unfulfilled desire in this season of your life. The person, the dream, the ideal that so much of your identity has been wrapped up in has been taken. Maybe it was stolen from you or maybe it walked out on you. Maybe you are still in shock because it happened unexpectedly or maybe you are slowly watching it die in front of your eyes. *Where does the love go now?* Where does the love go for a parent that is slowly slipping away from you? Where does the dream you carried your whole life, yet never fulfilled, go to? What do you do with all the unfulfilled hopes for the child (or brother, sister, friend) who took his/her own life? Where does the love stored up for the soulmate who never entered our lives go? Where does the hope for an ideal we carried for years, but got smashed up, go? Absence often makes the heart grow colder not fonder. Whatever the circumstance, whatever the loss, reality shouts at us *'it's gone'* and we are left to survive the unfolding story of a life that we don't want to be ours. This, I believe, is the saddest and emptiest feeling in our human existence – when our greatest hope in life is reduced to the impossibility of burning up the current script of our life-story and starting again. We don't get that option and it feels downright cruel. I remember the hatefulness of this place vividly. Below is another extract from my journal. It was a week after Lindsay passed away. This wasn't in the script. I remember saying out loud: 'God, this is my story and I don't want it to be.'

I heard nothing back.

> I sit in my 'new' bedroom, back in my mum and dad's house; my little sister's old bedroom, with a single bed, a few old photographs and cards Lins had sent me over the years, one of Lins's dresses lies on my bed and I am surrounded by cardboard boxes containing the

contents of our little house. I realize that I am 27 and a widower and, still in a state of shock, I ask the question, 'God, how did I get here?' And then I can't help but say to him, 'God all I tried to do was serve you.' I don't like the story I find myself in. I don't want this to be my story. I am still hoping this is all it is – a story – and one day God will give Lins back and my real life can start again. I don't want this to be my life. And yet I am powerless. I can't do anything. I just have to go with the emotions that this stinking journey of grief takes me on.

STAYING ALIVE ... JUST!

I would have described myself as a relatively vulnerable person before Lindsay's death but, like most people, I knew how to repress pain, how to manage insecurity, emotion and internal conflict. Lindsay's death afforded me no such opportunity. The pain was so overwhelming I simply couldn't control it. C.S. Lewis described his emotions swinging between resenting the profound pain of grief when he was experiencing it and anxiously waiting its return when he was not. This was not unlike the calm water with the distant thunder of the Nile rapids moving threateningly towards me. While the calm provided some degree of respite from the actual waves of grief, it was also the place where that dreadful, nervous, sick feeling of apprehension ate up my insides. What the next wave was going to be like I couldn't tell for sure, but I knew it was coming. Lewis described the ironic comfort he found while *in the middle* of a wave of grief for at least he knew what was happening to him at this moment. The foreboding and fear that shrouded the waiting was almost as horrible as the grieving itself.

I threw myself into my football training. I played semi-professionally and concentrated on getting as fit as I could for the new season ahead, hoping that it would bring some healing, a way to fulfill some other dream. But my body couldn't cope with it; just like my soul, it was going to take months to heal. Doctors later explained that our bodies are not built to deal with such extremes of trauma and pain. The brokenness of the soul is so severe that it manifests in physical pain and weakness lasting many weeks and months.

My football training included both aerobic and anaerobic exercise. During the preseason, footballers will undergo a gruelling regime of aerobic exercises to build strength and endurance for the long season ahead. Then, when the league starts, the training changes to focus on *anaerobic* exercise which concentrates on developing bursts of speed and power. Our coaches would order us through repeated sprints or other types of high intensity circuit training. These exercises led to a starving of oxygen in the muscle cells, causing them to rely on other reactions to fuel muscle contraction. Anaerobic training leaves you gasping for breath to fill up empty lungs on cold Tuesday and Thursday nights during the winter. Sharp but deep intakes of breath were needed to prevent lightheadedness, fainting or throwing up! Anaerobic exercise had been a weekly discipline for me for more than fifteen years and this part of the grief process reminded me of it – of the sensation of breathlessness due to the starvation of air. Every breath was a desperate gasp, sharp and deep, jabbing the heart. And yet, I knew my grief journey would last longer than a concentrated 90 minutes. Disturbingly, I was becoming aware, this journey was more like a long distance race, a long and arduous journey that would require a wholly different form of 'training' to get through, and I was only at the beginning.

Phil had taught me that 'walking helps', and it did. It helped me to process my thoughts and it eased the heaviness. It was a case of walking out the pain rather than letting it orbit around me. I contemplated praying but conversations with God at this stage mainly involved bargaining with him to give Lindsay back to me. On more than one occasion I pleaded with him that if he just give her back for five minutes, if he would allow me a brief apparition, I wouldn't tell anyone he had bent the rules for me. I walked along a beach at Cranfield, on Northern Ireland's County Down coast, and imagined that God might just place Lindsay behind a big rock at the end of the beach for a brief moment together. If he really loved me surely he would do this and no one would ever know.

Again, it seemed easier to write my thoughts to God rather than speak them. This was my prayer a week after Lindsay's death:

> 29th April 2007. Tonight feels like the dark night of the soul. It feels like I don't want to live anymore. Something/almost everything inside of me has died. I feel like a shell – a shell that just exists. Today feels like more of the harshness of the reality is kicking in and it is indescribable. The pain is so deep it feels difficult to breathe. It feels like my throat is dry and I am suffocating inside. It was a week this morning since Lins breathed her last and this seems to have brought on the next wave of grief. This hurt, deadness, harshness – a more acute reality … Sometimes I go through moments of verging once again on normality and 'then comes a sudden jab – a red hot memory'.[7] I cannot bear the thought of not seeing Lins again.

Each day felt like a year. The evenings were the worst. There were nights I simply didn't know if I would make it to the morning. The fact that I did was a miracle in itself. As Anne Lamott describes, 'the miracle is that we are here, that no matter how undone we've been the night before, we wake up every moment and we are still here'.[8]

I can still remember the feeling of tears running out of my eyes down into my ears. Phil had warned me of the 'tears in your ears' night sessions. To try to ease the intense feelings of loneliness and the longing to hold Lins again, my favourite dress of hers was my lifeless companion in bed for a number of weeks. I missed her body desperately. If you have been in this place before you will know the utter despair of trying to survive when you don't want to. If you are in this place at the moment, my heart breaks for you.

---

[7] Anne Lamott, *Stitches: A Handbook on Meaning, Hope and Repair*, Riverhead Books (2013).

[8] Anne Lamott, *Stitches: A Handbook on Meaning, Hope and Repair*.

Hang on.

It will get better.

But, yeah, I know, at the minute it hurts like hell.

Thought after thought and feeling after feeling which always had Lins as their object now have lost their target. So many roads (thoughts, feelings, emotions) led to Lins in my mind and they all appear to be dead ends now. 'Her absence is like the sky, spread over everything' (C.S. Lewis). Everything I do, she is there but then she isn't. I cannot phone her, tell her about what I am doing, text her, bring her something home. Just emptiness. This feeling of sickness right in the middle of me. At times this week I have had this paradoxical sensation where, at times when I have felt Lins closest (almost tangibly felt her beside me) she has also seemed further away than ever. These times are the worst. Horrible.

I am trying to begin the process of rebuilding my life again. But it is precisely at the point of feeling you are getting anywhere that I find myself back to square one, falling flat on my face and, back in this place of overwhelming emotional pain. Every time you think you are getting somewhere you feel like someone has pushed your head under water again and you are scrambling for air all over again. Relentless, successive emptiness.

I try to remember verses like this in these times:

'For you have seen my troubles, and you care about the anguish of my soul' (Psalm 31:7 NLT).

But trusting God has never been so hard … there is this fear that trusting him means allowing him to heal my heart and while I really want and need that, there is a part of me scared, as it could mean finding a way of doing life without Lins. Some moments I can come to a vague kind of acceptance of this, other days I can't. The cliché is right. One day at a time is all you can do.

Trusting God to get you to the end of the day. The future is full of fear when I try to think about it too much but the present is not much better, so I keep going one day, one hour, at a time ...

Even in the moments when grief subsided and the sharp pain was a little numbed, I tried to turn my eyes outward for some perspective, but I just didn't know how to 'be'. I simply did not know how to 'do life' anymore. My life was broken in a million pieces and without Lins the idea of even trying to put the pieces back together stirred an angry emotional reaction. As when two colours of plasticine get mixed together, it was impossible to separate us completely. When Lindsay died, large pieces of me went with her. The parts of *me* that had been woven into her in our short lives together *were still with her*. To separate us meant a violent ripping and tearing apart, leaving the edges exposed and vulnerable – like an open flesh wound. The oneness, the perfect completeness we had enjoyed, now left me half the man I was before. Death had broken the covenant we had embraced.

It was over.

A REFERENCE POINT: COMPANIONS OF LAMENT

Each heart knows its own bitterness, and no one else can share its joy.

Proverbs 14:10 NIV

During the early days of simply surviving, I found myself instinctively searching for someone who could 'get me'. I needed companions to help me read the map of this new terrain – the Valley of Weeping – I found myself in. I wasn't sure where I was going so I needed help to find at the very least a reference point, a starting point. There is a loneliness to these seasons of life that our original design was not created to experience, resulting in an insatiable desire to find connection somewhere: to simply find somebody who can 'get' the bitterness of my heart.

I didn't care what my future held at this stage, I just needed something or someone to tell me where I was. I found myself searching for people who would not try to fix me or force me to contemplate the future. I couldn't envisage a future without Lindsay, so I didn't need anyone pushing me into it. Rather I needed people, places, music that would just simply be with me in this place. Someone who could be present in my pain. Places that gave space for my emotions, music that resonated with my lonely misery. My companions in these 'survival days' came from unexpected places, mainly poets, writers and artists. The works and music of Elie Wiesel, C.S. Lewis, Anne Lamott, Bruce Springsteen, Ian Archer, Lies Damned Lies, Over the Rhine. They met me in this place of pain, doubt and confusion, articulating my broken soul in language and melodies that journeyed into the remoteness and edges of my broken heart. I felt a little less lonely when I read or listened to their words. I was disappointed by the lack of lament in much of contemporary Christian music and literature and observed a disproportionate focus on triumphalism and victory. Suffering, tribulation and doubt didn't seem to sell albums! Thankfully, I came to realize, this is not the case in the Bible. While I was unsure of how I could engage with God, I came to realize that the Bible was full of lament – songs, prayers and petitions of suffering and heartache. The anguish expressed in Jeremiah and Lamentations; the questions and wrestlings of Job; and the honest veracity of the Psalms were some of the ways I found a deep connection with the Bible. I discovered a new intensity, rawness, and emotion in the Bible I had previously missed. The cries in the writings of Jeremiah are a stark example of 'poured out' grief and he along with others became one of my soul companions, helping me make it through the day, setting up camp with me in the Valley of Weeping.

This is why I weep and my eyes overflow with tears. No one is near to comfort me, no one to restore my spirit. My children are destitute because the enemy has prevailed

Lamentations 1:16 NIV

Streams of tears flow from my eyes because my people are destroyed.

Lamentations 3:48 NIV

I have cried until the tears no longer come; my heart is broken. My spirit is poured out in agony.

Lamentations 2:11 NLT

Oh that my head were waters, and my eyes a fountain of tears, that I might weep day and night for the slain of the daughter of my people!

Jeremiah 9:1

The Psalms also became part of my staple diet. I (re)discovered this treasure buried in the middle of the Bible, the prayer book of the church for centuries, as language for my lamenting soul. In the future many of these sacred hymns and prayers would minister hope to me, but at this stage I wasn't ready for hope unless it involved some way that would bring Lindsay back. For now, though, I just needed words and people who would be *present* in my pain, not try to get me out of it. The Psalms didn't disappoint. Psalm 88 helped the most in the days of survival because it 'got me'. It contains not one glimmer of hope. Matthew Henry's description is accurate:

> This psalm is a lamentation, one of the most melancholy of all the psalms; and it does not conclude, as usually the melancholy psalms do, with the least intimation of comfort or joy, but, from first to last, it is mourning and woe.[9]

---

[9] Matthew Henry, *Commentary on the Whole Bible*, Thomas Nelson (1 May 2003).

God, you're my last chance of the day.
    I spend the night on my knees before you.
Put me on your salvation agenda;
    take notes on the trouble I'm in.
I've had my fill of trouble;
    I'm camped on the edge of hell.
I'm written off as a lost cause,
    one more statistic, a hopeless case.
Abandoned as already dead,
    one more body in a stack of corpses.
And not so much as a gravestone –
    I'm a black hole in oblivion.
You've dropped me into a bottomless pit,
    sunk me in a pitch-black abyss.
I'm battered senseless by your rage,
    relentlessly pounded by your waves of anger.
You turned my friends against me,
    made me horrible to them.
I'm caught in a maze and can't find my way out,
    blinded by tears of pain and frustration.

I call to you, God; all day I call.
    I wring my hands, I plead for help.
Are the dead a live audience for your miracles?
    Do ghosts ever join the choirs that praise you?
Does your love make any difference in a graveyard?
    Is your faithful presence noticed in the corridors of hell?
Are your marvelous wonders ever seen in the dark,
    your righteous ways noticed in the Land of No Memory?
I'm standing my ground, God, shouting for help,
    at my prayers every morning, on my knees each daybreak.
Why, God, do you turn a deaf ear?
    Why do you make yourself scarce?
For as long as I remember I've been hurting;
    I've taken the worst you can hand out, and I've had it.
Your wildfire anger has blazed through my life;

I'm bleeding, black-and-blue.
You've attacked me fiercely from every side,
    raining down blows till I'm nearly dead
    You made lover and neighbor alike dump me;
    the only friend I have left is Darkness.

Psalm 88 MSG

This was the language of my survival days, making it through the day with *darkness* – my closest friend. Life in these days was encompassed by 'mourning and woe'. Hope was an apparently ludicrous imposter. The metaphors of the Psalms provided helpful expressions of what could not be fully put into words. I was submerged underwater like David describes in Psalm 69 and I found these sacred words could give cogency, like no other, to my scrambled emotions.

Save me, O God,
for the waters have come up to my neck.
I sink in the miry depths,
    where there is no foothold.
I have come into the deep waters;
    the floods engulf me.
I am worn out calling for help;
    my throat is parched.
My eyes fail,
    looking for my God.

Psalm 69:1–3 NIV

Those who have not experienced such acute grief or deep pain may find my descriptions overly intense or even melodramatic. Part of my conviction for writing this book was to identify with the many people who are living through despairing days where it seems hope cannot even be comprehended. So my account of this stage of grief may seem overstated, unrestrained, but I assure you it is honest. Hope will look after itself if we can find a way to access and express our emotions honestly. The honest description of my survival days will, I hope, bring some level of validation to *your story* and

29

your journey of heartache and, in a small but hopefully significant way, bring solace. My encouragement to you through highlighting the scriptures above is – *God understands this place*. I know you might not be convinced yet, but stick with me. In Psalm 88 (and others) God gives us a language for days when darkness alone is our closest friend. It doesn't mean we get many answers at this point and we may not have even completely accepted our new cruel reality, but there is some succour in knowing you are understood – particularly by your Maker.

As I look back on those survival days, I remember the newfound appreciation I developed for the integrity and honesty of the scriptures. It was strange to me but I began to experience a kind of holy connection, a recognition that the Bible made space for such outbursts of utter hopelessness and pain. Without rushing me from this place, the words of sacred scripture rested on me and gave voice to my despair. I trust that you too may begin to experience such company in these sacred words from scared hearts.

Somehow, like my rafting experience on the River Nile, with help from these lamenting companions and secular saints, I just about managed to scramble back onto the raft, and then waited anxiously for what was around the next bend in the river. I was intimidated by the towering hillsides and the rumble and roar of the rapids ahead. While on my raft in Africa my fears were eased by the camaraderie of fellow team members, this time I felt alone, and utterly dwarfed by the size of the gargantuan waves in front of me. My frantic attempts at rowing through the rapids felt futile. But *I kept rowing*. Like the guides who urgently shouted instructions at us during our navigation of the Nile, directing us to row right into the middle of the next wave if we wanted to survive, so the Psalmists and others urgently shouted the words of lament to me. I began to realize that these unsung heroes of the faith knew how to navigate such times of monumental pain by 'rowing' right into and through the deep and dark waves. And this is how I would survive.

CHAPTER THREE

WHAT WILL YOU DO WITH YOUR PAIN?

One of my favourite TV personalities is Bear Grylls. He knows a thing or two about survival. He served in the Territorial Army and the SAS, climbed Mount Everest aged only 23, crossed the Atlantic in an inflatable boat. He has faced danger and hardships in deserts, in rainforests and on ice sheets. His thoughts on survival resonate with me. 'Survival is not about being fearless', he says. 'It's about making a decision, getting on and doing it, because I want to see my kids again, or whatever the reason might be.'[1]

Somewhere in the trial of simply making it through the day, a decision has to be made. In the melancholy haze of despair and broken dreams, pragmatism is an unwanted guest. Yet Bear articulates a truth and a strategy that is essential to avoid falling into the paralysis of utter despondency. Survival is about making a decision.

As I stared into the dark abyss of my future, utterly distraught, traumatized and scared, I saw that my future would be determined by my answer to one particular question. It was a question I didn't want to answer, but a question, I have come to realize, that we all must answer.

'What will you do with your pain? What will you do with your pain, Alain?'

This probing and haunting question, Richard Rohr argues, is the centerpiece of all great spirituality.[2] *What will you do with your pain?*

---

[1] Bear Grylls, interview with Oliver Smith in the *Daily Telegraph*, 9 November 2012.
[2] Richard Rohr, *Adam's Return: Five Promises of Male Initiation*, Independent Publishers Group (October 2004).

In the first stages of my grief, while still in denial, I refused to contemplate such an insensitive question. The thought of trying to embrace a future without Lindsay felt wrong. I had it all worked out: my love of Lindsay was so strong it would last the rest of my life. Then, one day, I was confronted by a startling question. My counsellor, Andrea, gently affirmed my profound and mysterious connection with Lindsay. But she said this: 'Alain, you are trying to find ways to keep yours and Lindsay's love alive so that it will get you through the rest of your life. And it can't.'

What will you do with your pain?

It was the hardest and wisest thing anyone had said to me. I had to answer the question, I had to make a decision. Going back wasn't an option. Nor was standing still.

I had to face my grief, stare it in the eye, confront it. This would mean unzipping my soul and letting pain work its way through me. This would mean, rather than running away, like Jonah, my decision to survive would begin with raising my hands and allowing myself to be thrown into the crashing seas, to be engulfed by waves of grief, to fall into the turmoil of the deep. The only way to survive this storm was, in what seemed a cruel twist of irony, to be thrown overboard.

I slowly raised my hands. As I made the decision, I didn't know whether it would kill me or not. But I knew that if I didn't, a worse kind of death would kill me inside. I might live physically but I would exist as a shell, growing old with a cynical and bitter heart. I was going to have to allow my pain to go through me and, in the light of God's face, let pain have its way with me.

Author Sarah Bessey explains this choice. She likens how we deal with the pain of life to the experience of women in childbirth going through the *fear – tension – pain* cycle. As labour approaches, the first reaction is fear. Fear leads to tension which causes more pain. Pain induces more fear and so the cycle continues, potentially sabotaging the new life. Sarah describes how her doctor encouraged her to 'lean into the pain' helping her to overcome the fear as she recognized the new birth that waited on the other side.

Childbirth provides an insightful metaphor for the cycle of emotions we experience in times of acute emotional pain. Like pregnancy, our journey through difficult seasons of life will be a very real *felt* agony but in learning to lean into the pain we can release it gradually as we remind ourselves of the coming now life

> Lean into the pain. Stay there in the questions, in the doubts, in the wonderings and loneliness, the tension of living in the Now and the Not Yet of the Kingdom of God, your wounds and hurts and aches, until you are satisfied that Abba is there, too. You will not find your answers by ignoring the cry of your heart or by living a life of intellectual and spiritual dishonesty. Your fear will try to hold you back, your tension will increase, the pain will become intense, and it will be tempting to keep clinging tight to the old life; the cycle is true. So be gentle with yourself. Be gentle when you first release. Talk to people you trust. Pray. Lean into the pain. Stay there and the release will come.[3]

THREE TRUSTED COMPANIONS

The only way I would truly grieve was by being me, by being honest with myself. The only way to be fully healed was to be fully present with the pain in my heart. If it's the truth that sets you free, I instinctively knew that the faint hope of freedom would come only with a full acknowledgement of my deepest and truest agonies. I needed to gently but courageously lean into the pain. This book is both a reflection and, I hope, a guide to what I have learned by doing this.

If you are walking a similar path, and as you read these words feel a tug on your heart, a challenging invitation to honestly respond to the question 'what will you do with your pain?', let me humbly introduce you to three pairs of companions as you begin to walk this inner pilgrimage.

---

[3] Sarah Bessey, *Jesus Feminist: An Invitation to Revisit the Bible's View of Women*, Howard Books, original edition (5 November 2013).

1. Journey and friends
2. Vulnerability and courage
3. Language and liturgy

Journey and friends

There was an image I kept seeing as I confronted the pain. I saw myself walking into a dark tunnel. I knew instinctively that the only way I could ever see the light was to keep walking – I had to take a long journey not knowing what was in front of me. Standing still would get me nowhere – inactivity meant staying in this living hell. I needed to start putting one foot in front of the other. Pilgrimage, I came to learn, is an art and a discipline, something our ancestors understood. In practical terms, some things have to be talked out, walked out and prayed out. Pilgrimage is the way to transformation.

Strangely, and slightly disconcertingly, walking through this tunnel and embracing the pain felt like an invitation from God. In the darkness I couldn't see his hand but sensed it there. There were no words, no real form, just an awareness of an outstretched hand and an invitation to journey with him.

In moving into the darkness, towards the darkest part of the tunnel, I was moving closer to the first streams of light. The brightness of the noonday sun was awaiting me on the other side. Initially, this reality was a far distant hope. From my current position it appeared as nothing more than a fragile and flickering candle, kept alive in my mind simply because of logic rather than faith. I had a long way to go and I knew it was likely to get worse before it got better.

Mike Riddell describes hauntingly, and with a potent mixture of metaphors, what the next part of the journey would look like:

> But the dark days are just beginning. Before you emerge into the light again you will be stripped to the core. You will rage and scream at God. You will retreat into a cocoon of sorrow and breathe in slow motion. The colour will drain from the sky and the meaning from life. As a plough tears through hard earth, your heart will be broken up. You will make friends with pain, nursing it as a child of your grief. Utter emptiness fills the earth and the valley appears to contain nothing but

the echo of your own cry. Surely God has left you. The road which seemed to be heading somewhere has become a dead end. A mocking maze with no exit![4]

What Riddell and others before him have found is that pain is overcome only by being acknowledged, and the way to acknowledge it is to walk *towards* it and then *right through* it. I found this deeply introverted pilgrimage was more effective and a bit less painful when I mirrored it with physical movement: walking around the park, driving nowhere in particular, flying to a different country. The outward geographical movement was almost a real-life analogy to the internal processing of pain and disorientation. As I moved around physically I could pay attention to my emotions and slowly begin the process of unravelling them. The earthy wisdom of uncle Phil's words gently encouraged me forward: 'Walking helps, Alain.'

One journey in the early days of my grief stands out in my memory. Five weeks after Lindsay died, my friend Brian called me. Brian had recently moved to Ibiza with his wife Tracy and two young sons to develop the work of 24-7 Prayer there, hosting summer mission teams to pray, bless and share Jesus with the clubbers on the notorious West End. Someone in the UK had generously offered to buy them a car for the ministry – for escorting drunk, drug-fuelled, vulnerable young people back to their hotels safely at night. Brian was flying to England to collect the car and called to ask if I would drive it out to Ibiza with him. I had no real reason to say no, figuring that it could only be good for me. For the next two days we journeyed through England, France and Spain. At times we chatted about football, at times we chatted about grief, at times we were silent and at other times we found a space to laugh.

On this journey, through every city and country, my grief came with me. I couldn't escape it. Journeying in these days of grief teaches

---

[4] Mike Riddell, *GodZone: A Guide to the Travels of the Soul*, SPCK (2010).

you that there are no hiding places. In my desperation, I recalled a distinct sense of disappointment when I realized the impossibility of escape. On every new road, around every corner, at every border, the emptiness followed. I remember noticing the road signs – Paris, Limoges, Bordeaux, Toulouse, Carcassonne, Barcelona – and for light relief I would match the football teams I had grown up watching on TV with the cities we were passing, or would laugh with Brian as we pronounced these cities phonetically in an exaggerated Northern Irish accent. Yet the grief, resolute and steady, kept coming with me.

The best way to describe this feeling is as an intense form of homesickness, only it was even worse because while I longed for 'home' I wasn't sure where 'home' was anymore.

> Over the last couple of weeks I have become more acutely aware of a feeling of homesickness. It is impossible to find the feeling of 'home' anywhere at present – that feeling of wholeness and completeness has gone, and as much as I desire to feel at home again, it seems that it cannot be found. Home is heaven, I have realized, and as it feels as if part of me has already been taken there, I find myself longing for God to wrap things up on this earth, allowing the new world to come into being, so that once again I might feel that sense of 'home' and wholeness. I think this feeling is even more real to me because the more I reflect on the last year the more I realize I had the deep, deep privilege of tasting something of heaven with Lins and I long for that feeling again. That feeling of 'home' – it's hard to put into words but I pray you know what I mean – the feeling of being settled and centred and completed in your soul. It leaves me feeling like a bit of an alien in this world at present – a wanderer, a nomad, a pilgrim, journeying through life seeking to find home. It is a complete paradigm shift, where the lens through which you looked at the world has been totally changed and the broader context of heaven frames your whole outlook on life. A friend

pointed out that Jesus was homeless too – nowhere to lay his head. He journeyed and wandered around on his mission before he returned 'home'.

In a strange, painful way I have a tiny glimpse of what it must have felt like.

Acknowledging this was difficult but, in hindsight, it was an essential part of the process. Although the grief came with me, although I could not escape it, and could not find home, I found in the physical action of traveling with a dear friend a space for grief to work through me. Simply gazing out the window at landscapes I hadn't seen before, or navigating French service stations and motels, provided novelty and healthy distraction. The monumental pressure squeezing down on me when I was at home lifted a little, allowing me to draw in deeper and longer breaths of air. I learned that journeying gave me a frame of reference to walk through my pain – whereas sitting in self-pity, intellectual reasoning or mystical oblivion would squeeze out any life left in me, like air pathetically squealing out of a balloon.

Journeying with Brian, chatting about our lives, both seriously and trivially, quite simply, helped. Brian had lost his mother when he was a young boy, and could relate to my pain. We didn't come up with any answers but there was solace in trusting the process together. That's the thing about any journey – it feels complete only in the presence of another. All the best movies, all the best epic stories, whilst drawing us into an overarching narrative, usually reveal that the real point is found as much in the means – in the relationships created and friendships fostered during the story – as in the end. I can't overstate the importance of fellow pilgrims on the journey through grief. The power of accessing your pain in the presence of trusted friends should not be underestimated. Good friends keep you alive.

As you lean into your pain, I would encourage you to journey. It will keep your heart beating, preventing the pain from paralyzing your over-analytical mind or from tormenting your disorientated soul. Walk, run, drive, fly. Keep moving – it is too sore to sit still. Journey, pilgrimage, sojourn. We are born to travel. The Creator has always been calling his image bearers on adventures on top of mountains and through deep gorges and valleys.

Find some trusted friends to walk with you. Remember that Jesus is walking with us, his presence keeping our heart burning even when we are still unsure it is him. I have an inkling that Jesus knows exactly what he is doing in these times. He knows we aren't ready to fully face him yet. He doesn't want to rush us until the pain does what it needs to with us. But he cannot resist being present with us.

As I journeyed through my own tale of survival, God gave my homesick soul a sign. He gave me friends. They know who they are. And he gave me the ability to walk beside them.

Vulnerability and courage

In his *New York Times* bestseller, *The Fault in our Stars*, John Green writes about the fictional life of Hazel Grace Lancaster, a 16-year-old terminally ill cancer patient, who falls in love with a fellow sufferer, and is left to mourn his death. Hazel's father offers his wisdom: 'Grief doesn't change you, Hazel, it reveals you.'[5] One thing I have come to understand is that grief *can* change us, but I do agree to some degree with this insight. Before grief changes us, it will *reveal* us, opening us up to parts of ourselves we didn't realize were there. Grief certainly did reveal me and it opened up others who were engaging with me on the journey. To my surprise, it seemed that my vulnerability was creating space for others. As I shared my pain, they seemed to be able to access their pain more naturally. I came to realize that not only does vulnerability carry astonishing power, it is also a most beautiful gift.

I find it fascinating how Green's work, written for teens, has captivated adults also. The book deals honestly with pain, suffering, death and grief and it is perhaps the underlying vulnerability pervading the book that captures the hearts of its many readers.

---

[5] John Green, *The Fault in Our Stars*, Penguin, black edition (3 January 2013).

Maybe it shouldn't be surprising, though, as many of the book's readers live in the superficial, hyped-up bubble of western civilization quietly desperate for something authentic and real, searching for someone else who can connect with the pain and suffering they are carrying in their hearts. Vulnerability is the connection. As the inspirational Madeleine L'Engle concluded, 'When we were children, we used to think that when we grow up we would no longer be vulnerable. But to grow up is to accept vulnerability. To be alive is to be vulnerable.'[6]

Contrary to the perception that vulnerability is associated with weakness, vulnerability is powerful, establishing the grounds for healing and love to be received. As Brené Brown proposes in *Daring Greatly*, vulnerability is more accurately synonymous with love and understood as 'uncertainty, risk and emotional exposure'.[7] We need to lose the negative associations with vulnerability and receive it as the beautifully courageous virtue it is. What's not risky about loving someone? What's not uncertain about making your feelings known? Anyone who has ever plucked up the courage to reveal his or her true feelings to another human being knows something of the risk involved. Vulnerability is not a weakness, it is plucky and gutsy and honest. It reveals to us what matters most in life, and in doing so connects us deeply with the common brokenness we share with our fellow human beings. Healthy vulnerability shines a light into the shadows and dispels something of the loneliness that we experience in our souls.

To navigate such times, we need to develop a counter-culture of vulnerability that encourages people not to deny their pain but to lean into their pain courageously. This does not mean people should be encouraged to see suffering as a virtue. Any form of self-pity or self-righteousness exercised in times of suffering is an indication that the suffering hasn't transformed us the way it was supposed to. Rather, we need to champion and authentically observe the courage it takes to embrace suffering honestly. Healthy vulnerability gives permission to

[6] Madeleine L'Engle, *Walking on Water*, Convergent Books (11 October 2016).
[7] Brené Brown, *Daring Greatly: How the Courage to be Vulnerable changes the Way We Love, Live, Parent and Lead*, Penguin Life (3 December 2015).

bring that grief, doubt, sin and pain into a safe place where it can be acknowledged and prayed!

The Greek term *persona* is translated 'stage mask'. Suffering forces us to choose whether we want to lose the 'persona', unmask ourselves and embrace the true person. The Greek root for the English word *passion* – which we often associate with romantic or sexual love – derives from *pashko*, which means 'to suffer'. Passion is not just about what you love, it is what you are willing to endure and suffer for. Putting the two ideas together: if we truly want to find ourselves (our true persona) in the midst of our losses we must be prepared to risk the uncertainty of vulnerability.

Language and liturgy

While vulnerability is the posture required to allow people to walk through the tunnel of grief, *language* is the food pilgrims need to survive the long walk towards the light. Dallas Willard, in his seminal book *The Divine Conspiracy*, contends that western contemporary Christianity's

> lack of adequate ideas and terminology does great harm to our faith. It insulates us from real life and what we say we believe ... to trust in God we need a rich and accurate way of speaking about him, to guide and support our life vision and our will. Such is present in Biblical language.[8]

During my own 'dark night of the soul' I started to realize that Willard was right. The words of scripture I had read many times before were not as prosaic and didactic as they previously appeared to me. I came to see that these parts of the Bible were powerfully filled with an emotion and honesty that broke through superficial religious stoicism and certitude. I came to realize that much of the Bible was nutrition for the soul in all of life's seasons.

What did the writers of the Bible do in times of grief, loss and suffering? What did they do with their pain? They did the most

---

[8] Dallas Willard, *The Divine Conspiracy*, William Collins (5 October 1998).

courageous thing of all – they prayed it. They prayed it all. The Psalmists in particular gave voice to doubt, confusion, anger and even hatred, forming them all as prayers. They are daring and unmistakenly imminate prayers and their words and would our lips to pray the prayers we never imagined ourselves praying. These prayers meet us in the loneliest and darkest places of our existence and keep us company as we walk through our own 'dark night of the soul'.

The Hebrew prayers of the Old Testament are much more veracious than our current western evangelical sub-culture of self-help, pop-Christianity. The Psalms have caressed the souls of millions through the centuries, providing a language for every emotional experience. At the heart of these sacred texts is: 'Don't be stoic! Weep it – call it for what it is, offer it all up to God.' These poems have proved to be the Church's most authentic, accessible and powerful hymnbook for centuries. We still need them today.

I came to find a deeper and more honest cry of the heart in the prayers of David, Job and Jeremiah than I did in modern liturgy or worship songs. They understood that pain was not something to be suppressed or a demon needing to be expelled. Pain was pain. It wasn't anything they desired but they knew it would come to human beings in a fallen world. For them it was often a sign their hearts were still beating. Part of being alive was to suffer pain and they chose to suffer it *before God*.

The ancient Hebrews' propensity to suffer is a lesson to us in the modern western world. We either run from pain in denial or try to control it with medication and willpower. Neither of these methods *deal* with pain. The Hebrews, like many tribal cultures today, accepted pain much more realistically than we. How? They endured it, they prayed it, they suffered it and they allowed it to transform them. They expected it and when it came they dealt with it spiritually in the fullest sense of that word. Before God, they knew that suffering was something they walked *through* not around, and journeyed *into* not escaped from. For these wandering pilgrims, a cry of pain was a cry of praise.

The Psalms refuse to pretend that everything is ok. They stay clear of moralizing and they won't settle for cute platitudes.

Emotional repression is never an option; partial gains cannot be accepted. The Psalms speak with candour, lucidity and passion about their experienced pain that reinforces the integrity of their words. Their words, read slowly and aloud, speak for themselves and speak for us.

> My heart is in anguish within me;
> the terrors of death have fallen on me.
> Fear and trembling have beset me;
> horror has overwhelmed me.
> I said, 'Oh, that I had the wings of a dove!
> I would fly away and be at rest.
> I would flee far away
> and stay in the desert;
> I would hurry to my place of shelter,
> far from the tempest and storm.'
>
> Psalm 55:4–8 NIV

I have seen a glimpse of this first-hand in rural communities in Africa. They too have taught me how to express pain and suffering with dignity and maturity. The words they use to comfort never sound trite or naïve for they have been schooled in the matrix of life's hardships in much more authentic ways than many in the west. Their lives speak to us about the certainty of experiencing pain in this life. They reveal to us the necessity and the privilege we have to express our response to pain in prayer. These beautiful people are for me modern day examples of the spirituality of the Psalms. They know that if something is inside you it needs to be expressed and it needs to be expressed to God. They know that human beings will only orbit around their pain until they pray it out before God. For them, all of life is prayer, not just the good bits.

I realized that while initially the Psalms were providing me a language for my soul when I couldn't find one for myself, in the moments where a flow of emotion rose up in me the Psalms were also becoming the source of inspiration I needed. The Psalms inspired my own personal inscription. And so began my healing habit of journaling my own soul language. I decided to write my own psalms.

> Father, what to do when darkness is your closest friend? Even the few moments of calm I do experience bring with them this feeling of no purpose or meaning to life. I don't want to have a life without Lins anymore. I can't and don't want to comprehend it. It does not seem fair. The feeling of losing 'the One', my 'One' is pulling the heart out of me. It seems like it is pulling your life out of me. For what we had was your life, your love in us. So now it feels like I have lost your life in me. Only you can fix it

The prayers that have affected my life the most, the ones that I remember the most, are those that were most honest. For the first fourteen years of my life I went to a little country gospel hall. Sunday morning services were purely centred on 'remembering the LORD'. Different men (only men were allowed to) thanked Jesus for his death and for forgiveness of sins. Many of these men would pray genuine, eloquent prayers of love for Jesus but most of them sounded the same. When my neighbour Tom prayed, though, I always took notice. Tom was a farmer, laid back, honest and hard-working, endearingly clumsy. He possessed the most wonderful smile and contagious laugh. His prayers didn't carry the religious hyperbole as the men schooled in the scriptures. He didn't quote as many verses or attempt the big Christian words (predestination, justification, sanctification) that the others did. He prayed from the depths of himself. Words stumbled out of his mouth but they flowed from a grateful heart. What he lacked in eloquence he made up for in passion and soul. His humble heart overflowed with love and thankfulness to Jesus for what he had done for him. Lacking pretence and religious jargon, Tom's prayers still live with me. I wanted to love Jesus like Tom did.

God is inviting us to bring our truest self to him. We need to worry less about what we are saying to him and more about *who* we are bringing to him – this is the genius of the Psalms.

WHAT WILL YOU DO WITH YOUR PAIN?

We return to the question, *what will you do with your pain?* Remember, survival is about making a decision. What will *you* do with *your* pain? The partner who has left, the lifelong friend who has betrayed you, the infertility you are coming to terms with, the parent who is slowly aging and dying, the singleness you are despising, the child who died far too young, the terminal sickness you are facing. I know what this pain feels like, but ultimately one way or another we still have to answer the question.

The reason I write this book is not to simply tell you my story but to humbly encourage those of you facing what seems like insurmountable grief and irreversible anguish to lean into the pain. You may feel like you have lost your life, but you don't have to lose your soul. Moving, allowing yourself to be vulnerable and giving voice to your pain will allow you to slowly overcome the fear which in turn will reduce the tensions and, although it feels like an absurdity now, bring forth something new. Once we deal with the fear, only then can we contemplate being fully healed, even changed. We don't know much in these broken and aimless days but we can be confident that as we lean into the darkness, unsure of where we are going, fear can be released and overcome.

> Even though I walk through the valley of the
> shadow of death,
> I will fear no evil, for you are with me;
>
> Psalm 23:4

There *is* light at the other end of the tunnel, there *is* hope, and there *is* more than you could ever imagine in this life and beyond. There are precious holy moments in the travail of a soul burning with pain. As I journeyed through my tunnel of grief, I experienced things I never thought I would, in places deep inside me I never thought existed.

I had to remap most of the boundaries of my previous world. The frontiers widened and I now have more capacity to love and be loved. I am more integrated, more free and ultimately I am more awed by the fact that I am alive

CHAPTER FOUR

THE PROTEST

Oh, night that guided me, Oh, night more lovely than the
dawn,
Oh, night that joined Beloved with lover, Lover transformed in
the Beloved!

St John of the Cross[1]

I have learned to kiss the wave that throws me against the
Rock of Ages.

Charles Spurgeon[2]

DISAPPOINTMENT WITH GOD

'I am disappointed in you' are words we dread hearing. Whether voiced by parents in response to an act of immaturity, a friend after an argument, or a teacher or colleague questioning your commitment, these words can cut like a knife. Loaded with subjective force and personal dissonance, they can touch a deep nerve, launching waves of shame and regret. A distance develops, and we then have to begin a journey of repairing the damaged relationship and rebuilding

---

[1] St John of the Cross, *Dark Night of the Soul*, Dover Publications Inc (28 April 2003).
[2] Charles Spurgeon, source unknown.

broken trust. We don't like to hear these words and, if we truly love someone, we don't like to say them either. The stronger the love that exists between two people, the deeper the emotional wounding and the greater the challenge to reconcile. As C.S. Lewis put it, 'If you love deeply you are going to get hurt badly.'[3]

But what do you do when you are disappointed with God? What do you do when, more than simply asking 'Why?' you are feeling that *'Why God?'* as a passionate rage in your very bones? John Stott cites Joseph Parker, minister of City Temple from 1874 until his death in 1902, as a stark example of a Christian leader raging against God:

> He says in his autobiography that up to the age of sixty-eight he never had a religious doubt. Then his wife died and his faith collapsed. 'In that dark hour,' he wrote, 'I became almost an atheist. For God had set his foot upon my prayers and treated my petitions with contempt. If I had seen a dog in such agony as mine, I would have pitied and helped the dumb beast; yet God spat upon me and cast me out as an offence – out into the wilderness and the night black and starless.'[4]

Questions

As I began to lean into the pain I became aware that the most acute emotion I was feeling was disappointment. Walking into the darkest part of this tunnel, where the ache of Lindsay's absence lingered most deeply, I was distressed: *why was she allowed to die?* Any answers seemed nebulous, inadequate and redundant. I was starting to accept she *was* gone, but I couldn't accept *why*. It would have taken only a word, or a breath, from God and she would have been completely healed. So why had he sat on his hands?

The torment of this place was intensified by my love for God. It would have been easier if I didn't believe in God and easier still if

---

[3] C.S. Lewis is credited with saying this. He may not have said these exact words though he probably would have agreed. The character that played Lewis in the movie *Shadowlands*, based on the love and loss he experienced with his wife, H, did quote these words.

[4] John R.W. Stott, *The Essential John Stott: The Cross of Christ*, InterVarsity Press (1999).

I didn't like him. Then it would have made sense, and I wouldn't have had to go through this process. But I loved God. I had pretty much always loved God. I had come to know him as a loving heavenly Father, One of my passions in life had been communicating his 'Father-heart' to a 'fatherless generation' but now it seemed he wasn't showing himself to be a good Father to me. I had loved him all my life, served him and tried my best to honour him. I had *waited* for Lindsay. She was the one I completely gave myself to. It felt like I had kept my side of the promise and now he had let me down. He hadn't come through for me. The hurt and disappointment was compounded by confusion and turmoil of mind because, no matter how much I felt let down by God, I knew he still loved me. But this didn't feel like love.

So why, God?

Why?

Faith unravelled

When I was a young boy, my mum often quoted 1 Samuel 2:30 to me: 'those who honour me I will honour'. When I was ten years old, the football team I played for trained on a Monday night. Unfortunately, this was the same night as the 'Monday Night Meeting', a children's meeting in the little church I was brought up in. You can guess where the allegiance of a 10-year-old football fanatic lay on Monday nights! Mum let me make the decision myself, but she premised it with the verse 'those who honour me, I will honour'. She taught me that if I put God first in my life, I could be sure he would honour me. And it worked! Even though I didn't go to training I still got picked for the team every Saturday. This pattern of thinking and theological reasoning was imprinted in my young heart, and I held to this principle through life. If I obeyed God I could expect his blessing, and if I didn't, then I couldn't complain if things didn't go my way. 'You reap what you sow, don't you?' 'Honour God and he will honour you,' became my mantra, and gave me strength through the challenging teenage years.

When Lindsay died, this theological underpinning completely fractured, crashing down all around me. I felt I had done a pretty good job of honouring God, but he hadn't kept his side of the deal. Surely I

49

deserved to be honoured. I had waited all my life for my soulmate and he had given me twenty-two months with her. *What?* I had sowed good seeds in life and as a result, reaped the death of my wife. And what about Lindsay? The seeds she had sown included faithfulness, acts of justice, godliness, kindness. She had been a faithful sister, a committed friend, a daughter who had honoured her parents, an advocate for the poor, and a lover of Jesus. All the verses in the Bible that appear conditional for the blessings of long life, health and prosperity, Lindsay had obeyed. The result – death at 23! Lindsay, at 23 years of age, should never have had to go through what she did, and every moral fibre in my body screamed 'It's wrong that she should die, it's just plain wrong.'

And why was I left? Left to simply survive the onslaught of merciless grief? I was ashamed of myself for being so selfish but I couldn't help feeling that it was just as unfair to leave me here, as it was to allow her to be taken at such a young age.

For a person who likes to have the cognitive components of faith squared and resolved, this was a tormenting period. It just didn't make sense and the fact I couldn't work it out only intensified the torture. I had hit an impasse with God and I couldn't see how it would be resolved. It wasn't that I threatened to abandon my belief in God, or even that I loved him any less. I was just so extremely disappointed in him. The only way I could deal with this disappointment was to tell him. I couldn't settle for withdrawing from this deadlock with God through some weak and benign form of acceptance. I needed to *pray* my disappointment. I needed to look into his eyes and *say* it.

But how could I? My ecclesiastical conditioning told me it was wrong, irreverent to express such prayers to God. And yet, discon-certingly, I had a feeling that these honest prayers might be the prayers my Father actually *wanted* me to pray. To pray what I thought I ought to pray at this moment – rather than what was real, what was actually going on inside me – would be disingenuous and contrived. It would feel sickeningly fake, what Richard Foster describes as 'ethereal, decarnate spirituality'.[5]

---

[5] Richard Foster, *Prayer: Finding the Heart's True Home*, Hodder & Stoughton (11 December 2008).

I knew I was too open with my emotions to keep my disappointment hidden, and I was aware of the truth in the proverb 'pain that isn't transformed will be transmitted'. If I tried to suppress it and just deny it, I would slowly die inside and somewhere down the line someone would feel the full force of my disappointment. Hurt people hurt people. I didn't want to be that person. I needed to pray my hurt. The Psalms affirmed my inclinations not to 'bottle it up' and the unhealthy consequences that would come if I remained silent.

> For when I kept silent, my bones wasted away
> through my groaning all day long.
>
> Psalm 32:3

> I pour out my complaint before him; I tell my trouble
> before him.
>
> Psalm 142:2

I couldn't stay silent. The prayers recorded in the Psalter became antiphonal to my own aching prayers of hurt and disappointment. They encouraged me to pour out my own personal complaint, protest and lament.

> Father, it pains me to say this but the frustration that I feel the last couple of days has led me to feel a sense of disappointment in you. It hurts me so much even to say this but I feel so hurt myself tonight. I can't imagine telling my own dad that I was disappointed in him never mind you. I don't want to hurt you for I love you. I believe you are a Father of mercy and compassion who loves his children. I have always believed that but I feel such disappointment with the restraint you showed towards Lindsay. Help me be honest with you, Lord, but I don't want to hurt you. I just don't understand why it had to be this way. Why I could not have got more time with Lins? I miss her and loved her so much.

These prayers of complaint, I learned from the Psalmists, were not just one-off, shallow ways of getting something off your chest, they were a perpetual lament: pouring out day after day, as wave after wave of disappointment passed through the deepest parts of me.

> Evening and morning and at noon
> I utter my complaint and moan.

> Psalm 55:17

I found these sacred and ancient laments gave me words to describe my *physical* anguish:

> My wounds stink and fester
> because of my foolishness,
> I am utterly bowed down and prostrate;
> all the day I go about mourning.
> For my sides are filled with burning,
> and there is no soundness in my flesh.
> I am feeble and crushed;
> I groan because of the tumult of my heart.
> O Lord, all my longing is before you;
> my sighing is not hidden from you.
> My heart throbs; my strength fails me,
> and the light of my eyes – it also has gone from me.

> Psalm 38:5–10

And they voiced the deep *emotion* of injustice and disappointment I was holding against God:

> All this came upon us,
> though we had not forgotten you;
> we had not been false to your covenant.
> Our hearts had not turned back;
> our feet had not strayed from your path.
> But you crushed us and made us a haunt for jackals;
> you covered us over with deep darkness.

> Psalm 44:17–19 NIV

I had no shortage of lament Psalms to keep me company and they inspired me to write my own. In the company of these ancient sages I let it all out. I let it fall out *before* the face of my Father, I protested to God.

MY PROTEST

I voiced my disappointment in the blog I wrote at this time.

> During the past week, for the first time in my life, I have had a very real experience of being disappointed with God. I have worked through this a little as the week went by – but it is such an unfamiliar, distant and heartbreaking place to be. I know that God can handle this but it hurts me so much to say it. It hurts me because this is the God I have loved from when I was a boy; this is the God who I have come to experience as Abba; my heavenly Father whose love I have experienced intimately in the depths of my soul and for the first time in my life this past week I felt genuinely disappointed in him. I think about how it might make my own dad feel if I told him I was disappointed with him, how much more with God – my Heavenly Father? It is not a nice place. Before I try to express this disappointment I want to repeat what I mentioned in earlier posts. I am genuinely thankful to God for what he gave me with Lins. I know everything I have in life is from him – his grace and provision. I feel so blessed to have got to enjoy the time Lins and I shared and to experience a depth of love, especially over the last seven months, that I never thought was possible. I know that it is so painful now because it was so good ...
>
> But I have so many questions, hurt and disappointment. I don't want to be the inspirational superhero Christian who just says all the 'right things', accepts the spiritual clichés and 'God is in control' answers. I can't. I don't

want to tell you stuff over the next few weeks about how God heals my broken soul (hopefully) if I can't tell you the stuff I struggle with presently because at the minute it is hard to even ask God to heal me. I feel I need to be true to what I am feeling and even though it hurts me to say this, I know that God wants me to express this disappointment – this disappointment at times with him. I have told God this. I think it is better to pray badly than not pray at all and so what I am saying and going to say is all in the form of a prayer – groans I have tried to find some words for and express to God.

This past week my feelings have moved to sheer disappointment with God. Disappointed that the woman I prayed for and waited for in a way that I thought honoured God, I only got just over a year and a half of marriage with. Disappointed that I did not get longer with the woman who, before God I committed myself to for the rest of my life. Disappointed I could not have got even a few more years longer with ...

I know in theory that God is not supposed to give his children second best and that he does not short-change us. But today it feels like he has. I thought we could have got longer together ...

I still believe in God, I still love God and I still plan to serve him with my life and I know he is the only one who can fix me – I just feel disappointed with him today.

I was in too far with God to accept a passive or general answer. I needed him to know how I felt. As much as it broke my heart to say this to God – my Father – I knew I had to. It was a horrible and perplexing place. In one ear I heard permission to express my disappointment but in the other ear I heard confusion and contradiction – why would God want me to tell him that I was disappointed in him?

JOB'S PROTEST AND ACCEPTANCE

To my surprise I found that protest in suffering is found often in passages of the Bible, perhaps in the story of Job more than anywhere else.

Job was a righteous man who, like me, loved God, but who, in ways even more devastating than mine, lost everything. I found a friend in Job, not just because, like me, he had lost his wife but because, like me, he asked 'Why?' He raged 'Why?' Job gave me the courage not to settle for clichés, or well-meaning yet shallow platitudes from observers. As Peterson describes in his introduction to the book of Job in *The Message* Bible, Job 'refused to let God off the hook' but rather 'took his stance before God'[6] and protested! It is this courage and the sheer audaciousness of Job's prayers that makes him one of the Bible's heroes.

Before my own tragedy I think I had a patronizing sense of sympathy for Job, but now I see him as one of the most daring characters in history. The righteous man who lost everything and, despite the advice of the intelligentsia, stood before the God of the heavens and told him exactly how he felt. He resisted the certitude and moralizing of his friends so that he could remain true before his Maker. Job's friends talked to others *about* God. Job talked *to* God.

This was simple prayer, but don't be deceived by the word 'simple' – simple prayer is the most courageous of all. Simple prayer is praying as you can and not as you can't or, as C.S. Lewis says, to 'lay before him what is in us and not what ought to be in us'. I love Peterson's argument that Job is not just a witness to the dignity of suffering in God's presence but also a protest against religion that has reduced suffering to explanations and 'answers'.

God gives us the gift of Job's story because he doesn't want us to settle for censored, impressive prayers. Don't lose touch with the

---

[6] Eugene H. Peterson, *The Message: The Bible in Contemporary Language*, NavPress (2002).

reality of your soul. Don't settle for technical arguments, gimmicks and labels. Let it all fall before his face and remember, as Nicholas Wolterstorff says in his beautifully tragic *Lament for a Son*, 'Every lament is a love song.'[7]

Like many life experiences, Job's suffering was undeserved, and it is exactly this that makes it so shocking, so confounding. It is outrageous that 'innocent' (the Bible describes him as 'godly' or 'righteous') Job should suffer on such a scale. Yet in the midst of unimaginable sorrow, Job refuses to settle for a resigned acceptance. Job protests.

> What did I do to deserve this?
> … I expected good but evil showed up.
> I looked for light but darkness fell.
> My stomach's in a constant churning, never settles down.
> Each day confronts me with more suffering.
> I walk under a black cloud. The sun is gone.
> I stand in the congregation and protest.
> I howl with the jackals.
>
> Job 30:24–29A MSG

Job *howls*. Think for a moment about the noise of jackals and wolves as they howl and shriek in the dark of night. This is how Job describes his agonizing protest. This is prayer.

Within these howling prayers, he articulates his pain and rage, his doubt and disappointment. Job's story reminds us that life does not conform to our tidy categories and compartments, our rational certitudes, even though many – like Job's friends – would seek to tell us it does. Barbara Brown Taylor captures it adroitly: 'When we encounter God in the cloud (of darkness and unknowing), certainties become casualties … faith has more to do with staying fully present to what's standing right in front of you than being certain.'[8]

These are wise words but, as many survivors of a shipwrecked life will testify to, they are incredibly tough to practise when our vacillating

---

[7] Nicholas Wolterstorff, *Lament for a Son*, Eerdmans (1987).
[8] Barbara Brown Taylor, article: *The Bright Cloud of Unknowing* via http://day1.org/369-the_rev_barbara_brown_taylor, 2 March 2014.

emotions are craving answers. This kind of pressure for certitude and absolutes, Brueggemann contends, is a frightened response to pain and subsequently means we never pray what we are actually feeling. The church in the West, Brueggemann observes, possesses an inability to engage with such disconcerting places: 'It is a curious fact that the church has, by and large, continued to sing songs of orientation in a world increasingly experienced as disorientated.'[9] I agree. The fact that we go on singing 'happy songs' flies in the face of what the writers of the Bible practised. Of course we want to lean towards joy and hope, and the Psalmists teach us this too, but they do not gloss over the pain. They give us permission to be real. No emotion for them was inappropriate to bring before God in prayer and worship. Nothing needed to be filtered for Yahweh's ears, nothing needed to be toned down, nothing, they would argue, should be withheld. Rage. Disappointment. Anguish. Hatred. Good worship brings the whole story into the picture.

> Everything must be brought to speech, and everything brought to speech must be addressed to God, who is the final reference for all of life.[10]

24-7 PRAYER

One of the privileges of my life is playing an active role in the 24-7 Prayer movement – the 'accidental' movement of prayer, mission and justice that began in 1999 on the south coast of England in a small, messy prayer room, inspiring a fresh wave of creative prayer and catalyzing cutting-edge mission in some of the most broken parts of the world. I got swept up in this crazy movement in its early years which was around the same time as I started to date Lindsay.

---

[9] Walter Brueggemann, *Spirituality of the Psalms*, Fortress Press, abridged edition (16 November 2001).
[10] Walter Brueggemann, *Spirituality of the Psalms*.

Some friends and I hosted a prayer room for young people in our home town. Many of them encountered God in profound ways, and then compassionate and missional acts began overflowing out of the prayer room and onto the streets. I shared our story around the country and took a leadership role in 24-7 Ireland. We witnessed a hunger in many churches for a culture of prayer and the prioritization of the presence of God at the heart of their communities.

Today, seventeen years later, we know of over 15,000 prayer rooms that have taken place in churches and nightclubs and almost everything in between. These prayer rooms are a wonderful modern-day reflection of the indiscriminate prayer this chapter is espousing. I never fail to be captured by the opportunity prayer spaces have provided for real dialogue with the Father – honest questions and disappointments pouring out from broken hearts. The disappointments that haunt us, the questions that tie us up in knots, the confusion that prevents us from engaging with God. Remember Peterson's advice: 'It's better to pray badly than not to pray at all.'[11] What we often perceive as our 'bad' prayers are in fact the heart of prayer itself. The prayers we pray from our most disappointed place are the best prayers of all.

I know a businessman who loves to take the 3 am slot in a prayer room because he says he likes the idea that when everyone else is sleeping he can come into a prayer room and shout. I know of a little boy who scribbled on a post-it note on a prayer wall in a school classroom 'Why did my little sister die?' and a teenage girl who heartbreakingly inscribed 'Why am I ugly?' on a piece of cardboard. These gutsy, authentic prayers are the kind of prayers that seem more in line with the Old Testament authors than many Sunday morning worship songs or liturgies. Honest protest and pain.

My friend, and our inspirational leader in the 24-7 Prayer movement, Pete Greig, in his book *God on Mute*, sums up the heart of 24-7 Prayer, and my reflections in this chapter, as he quotes Dorothee Solle:

---

[11] Eugene H. Peterson, *Answering God: Psalms as Tools for Prayer*, Bravo Ltd (15 August 1991).

> If people cannot speak about their affliction they will be destroyed by it, or swallowed up by apathy … without the capacity to communicate with others there can be no change. To become speechless, to be totally without any relationship, that is death."

In my darkest days I learned to protest. I realized that no amount of prayer ministry was going to make my disappointment go away. My love for God seemed to be pushing me to fight him. If my relationship with him was going to continue beyond this pain I was going to have to wrestle with him like Jacob. I was going to have to wrestle him alone in the dark, with all the force within me I was going to *give him all my disappointment.*

So in the nights when most other people were sleeping, I would protest. I would have it out with God in the dark, one-on-one, toe-to-toe with my Maker. Sometimes walking the roads shouting at the heavens, other times weeping out my questions and disbelief as I lay on my bed. I would ask him my questions, I would offer my complaints, I would cry my tears in his face, I would cling to his arms, and even when I heard no answer I would not let him go.

WRESTLING – NORMAL, GOOD, INTIMATE

Frederick Buechner's incredible book on Jacob's life, *The Son of Laughter*, describes the intensity of Jacob's wrestle with the Angel of the Lord in Genesis 35:

> Out of the dark someone leaped on me with such force that it knocked me onto my back. It was a man. I could not see his face. His naked shoulder was pressed so hard against my jaw I thought he would break it. His flesh was chill and wet as the river … I got my elbow into the pit of his throat and forced him off. I threw him over onto his back. His breath

---

¹² Pete Greig, *God on Mute: Engaging the Silence of Unanswered Prayer*, Kingsway Publications, 1st paperback edition (4 April 2007).

was hot in my face as I straddled him. His breath came in gasps. Quick as a serpent he twisted loose and I was caught between his thighs. The grip was so tight I could not move. He had both hands pressed to my cheek. He was pushing my face into the mud, grunting with the effort. Then he got me on my belly with his knee in the small of my back. He was tugging my head up toward him. He was breaking my neck ... just as my neck was about to snap, I butted my head upward with the last of my strength and caught him square. For an instant his grip loosened and I was free. Over and over we rolled together into the reeds of the water's edge. We struggled in each other's arms. He was on top. I was on top. I knew they were not Esau's arms. It was not Esau. I did not know who it was. I did not know who I was. I knew only my terror and it was as dark as death. I knew only that the stranger wanted my life. For the rest of the night we battled in the reeds with the Jabbok roaring down the gorge above us. Each time I thought I was lost, I escaped somehow. There were moments when we lay exhausted in each other's arms the way a man and woman lie exhausted from passion. There were moments when I seemed to be prevailing. It was as if he was letting me prevail ... we could not see each other. We spoke no words. I did not know why we were fighting. It was like fighting in a dream. He outweighed me, he out-wrestled me, but he did not overpower me. He did not overpower me until the moment came to overpower me. When the moment came, I knew that he could have made it come whenever he wanted. I knew that all through the night he had been waiting for that moment. He had his knee under my hip. The rest of his weight was on top of my hip. Then the moment came, and he gave a fierce downward thrust. I felt a fierce pain. It was less a pain I felt than a pain I saw. I saw it as light. I saw the pain as a dazzling bird shape of light. The pain's beak impaled me with light. It blinded me with the light of its wings. I knew I was crippled and done for. I could do nothing but cling now. I clung for dear life. I clung for dear death. My arms trussed him. My legs locked him. For the first time he spoke, 'Let me go.'[13]

I never did get the answers I was looking for, but I didn't let go. More accurately he never let go of me. As I reflect on this time I realize that while I didn't get what I was originally looking for, I got more than I

---

[13] Frederick Buechner, *The Son of Laughter*, HarperOne (1994).

could ever have imagined. I got him. I was closer to him than I ever have been before. Even as I re-read Buechner's account of Jacob's encounter with the heavenly intruder, an emotion rises up within me reminding me of the most painful but intimate times with the 'Angel of the Lord'. It really is difficult to find words to describe the mysterious sacredness of such an encounter. At the time it was much more about endurance than enjoyment, but I sometimes wish I could bottle the depth of intimacy experienced in those dark nights and bring it into the present. Richard Rohr captures the mystery of this: 'the gift of darkness draws you to know God's presence beyond what thought, imagination or sensory feeling can comprehend.'[14]

When I was a boy, one of my favourite things was to wrestle with my dad. We would push the furniture back in the living room and make sure anything breakable was out of the way. Then it was game on! I would jump on my dad's back, try to get him in a headlock, grip his arms and hands tightly, hoping with childlike naïvety I could get him to submit to the 'pain' I was inflicting. In my mind it was a wrestle of epic proportions and I loved my dad for it; his energy was channelled towards me and the chance to give mine back to him made me feel like I was strong and confident. When he went to break free from my grip, I would respond with a stern 'NO!' I wasn't letting go and so he would play on. He would never be genuinely intimidated by my 10-year-old 'strength' but I know he enjoyed the closeness of these moments. Even though we both knew he could easily win, he kept allowing me to fight, kept allowing me to be close to him. When it came time to tame my over-exuberance and stop (usually on orders from Mum) he would exert his strength that little bit more forcefully. It was then I knew it was over. We had to stop and I had to go to bed. But the wrestle usually finished with a few moments when we lay exhausted in each other's arms, tired but aware of the strange intimacy we had just enjoyed and endured. It was a fight in my 10-year-old mind but, more accurately, it was love.

---

[14] Richard Rohr, *Richard Rohr's Daily Meditation: Luminous Darkness* (Monday 20 October 2014).

I have come to realize that God is not intimidated by anything we need to bring before him in prayer. Rather he calls us and invites us to wrestle with him because that is exactly where he wants to meet us. He longs for us to know that he meets us there and that he can take the verbal battering we direct towards him, especially if this means that afterwards we will fall completely into the security of his loving arms. The 'Angel of the Lord' towers above our problems, our sin, our pain.

> Cast your burden on the LORD,
> and he will sustain you;
> he will never permit
> the righteous to be moved.
>
> Psalm 55:22

He might not give you an answer but he promises to give you himself.

Peniel

As I meditated on Jacob's wrestling match with God, it became more obvious to me why he named the place Peniel, 'face of God'. Especially when I learned that in Hebrew, the 'face of God' was synonymous with the idea of his presence. The most common word for 'presence' in the Old Testament is *panim* which can also be translated 'face'. The German theologian Jürgen Moltmann explains the connection: '"the face of God" is a symbol for God's commitment, the attention with which he looks at us, and his special presence.'[15]

Can you see the beautiful thread of thought? The most intimate metaphor God uses to describe his presence is his face.[16] When God talks about his presence he is not talking about a vague, theoretical awareness of him. He is talking about his face. It couldn't be any

---

[15] Jürgen Moltmann, via Twitter, https://twitter.com/moltmannjuergen.
[16] A further example of how 'presence' and 'face' interchange in this passage: *Then he said to him, 'If Thy presence* [paniym] *does not go with us, do not lead us up from here. For how then can it be known that I have found favor in Thy sight, I and Thy people? Is it not by Thy going with us, so that we, I and Thy people, may be distinguished from all the other people who are upon the face* [paniym] *of the earth?'* Exodus 33:15–16 NASB 1977.

more personal. This connection between God's presence and his face is magnified intensely in one of my favourite passages of scripture, Exodus 33. Moses, who has led the Hebrew slaves out of Egypt and through their wilderness sojourn is now courageously bargaining with Yahweh to remain with them, to promise his continual presence on their journey into the promised land. God reveals himself to us in these pages as a broken and wounded lover. Grieved by the stiff-necked nature of his people, it seems the story is hanging in the balance – enough is enough and God declares he is not going with them. Distraught, Moses forcefully and passionately reminds God of his promises and their desperate need for his presence. His literal pitch to Yahweh is, 'unless your face goes before us we are not going'. As we read the narrative, we are left feeling like a spectator observing with an air of suspense. We wait nervously for God's response to Moses' stubborn refusal to move on without him. Moses drives a hard bargain – despite his people's constant disobedience, he will not make a deal to go anywhere, without God's total commitment of his most intimate presence. Incredibly, God concedes: reaffirming his commitment to his people and his willingness to continue his journey with them in the light of his presence, his face.

Moses' courageous heart-to-heart encounter with Yahweh and Jacob's wrestle with the towering Angel of the Lord in the eeriness of night carry a kind of holy fear. In both cases it seems they could have gone too far in engaging the way they did with this Almighty God. It seems like anything could happen. Jacob could be finished off by God for wrestling him and not being willing to give up and Moses potentially banished from God along with the rest of the Israelites for crossing the line, protesting too much and challenging God on his own nature! Yet both Jacob and Moses got more than they bargained for, for daring to protest to God. 'I have seen God face to face, yet my life has been spared.' More than simply making it through, they got the very face of God. Their stories imply we can too. This was the prayer I wrote in my journal during those fiercely intense nights:

> Father, as I read about Jacob wrestling with you I noticed how he sent everyone else over the brook and left himself on the other side of the

river with only you there left to fight. I have noticed that this is what it feels like for me. I am standing on the one side of a chasm, the rest of the world on the other side. Maybe everyone feels like this at some point in life and it is here we must wrestle until you bless. Jacob called this place Peniel which meant literally that he had met face to face with you. LORD, let it be for me. Teach me, Father, what it is that is born in suffering. What is it about this redemption that is mysteriously beautiful? What is it about hope that is born in pain? Father, I will not let you go until you bless me, until you meet with me, until you reveal yourself to me and like Jacob I can call this place Peniel – for I have met you face to face! Reveal yourself to me – meet me in this broken place – you have promised to be close to me. Flood me with your gentle touch and loving presence. God of comfort, I need you now – face to face. Meet with me.

FACE HIM

Whatever unresolved grief you are carrying, whatever trauma is in your bones, whatever insurmountable disappointment you are facing, there is an invitation from the Father to push back the chairs in the living room and lovingly embrace him in a wrestle. My humble encouragement to you is to engage, cry your tears *before* his face, write your own lamenting Psalm in the light of his presence, shout out your anger and shake your fists if you have to but make sure you are facing him when you do. It may not give you all the answers you are seeking – as Elie Wiesel said: 'I still have questions for God and I still have problems with God. But it is within faith, not outside of faith and surely not opposed to faith.'[17] Don't let anyone tell you this is irreverent or a lack of faith. This is what faith is all about. Whatever you have to do, just don't turn your back. Nothing you have to say intimidates him.

Meditating on his goodness and remembering his past acts of provision is a worthy discipline to continue in times of disappointment.

---

[17] Elie Wiesel, part of a speech made during an annual visit to the Chapman College in Orange County, California.

But don't allow this to be a cover for what really needs to be said, for, if our worship is truly to be 'in spirit and truth', everything should be poured out. Every part of us. God may be silent but don't you be!

You will find as you duel with the Angel of the Lord that the howling questions filling up your soul will get the hearing you feel they deserve. Gradually the raging within you will strangely quieten as you experience the tenderness emanating from his face. The protest you express allows the pain and torment in your mind to catch up with the pain in your heart.[18] God knows this and as a good Father, he just wants to hold you in the process, eventually stilling your soul as the emotion subsides. God, like all good lovers, knows true love is worth fighting for, worth dying for. The most difficult of nights can become the most intimate of nights; the night of greatest loneliness can become the night of life-changing encounter; the night of greatest struggle can give way to the day of deepest liberation and the place of seeming defeat can become the birth place for new life. Don't let him go until he blesses you.

Protest!

---

[18] Leslie C. Allen, *A Liturgy of Grief: Pastoral Commentary on Lamentations*, Baker Academic (2011).

CHAPTER FIVE

PATHOS

The deep of my profound misery calls to the deep of your
infinite mercy.

Bernard of Clairvaux[1]

If we have never sought, we seek Thee now;
Thine eyes burn through the dark, our only stars;
We must have sight of thorn-pricks on Thy brow;
We must have Thee, O Jesus of the Scars.
The heavens frighten us; they are too calm;
In all the universe we have no place.
Our wounds are hurting us; where is the balm?
LORD Jesus, by Thy Scars we claim Thy grace.
If when the doors are shut, Thou drawest near,
Only reveal those hands, that side of Thine;
We know today what wounds are; have no fear;
Show us Thy Scars; we know the countersign.
The other gods were strong, but Thou wast weak;
They rode, but Thou didst stumble to a throne;
But to our wounds only God's wounds can speak,
And not a god has wounds, but Thou alone.[2]

Edward Shillito

---

[1] Bernard of Clairvaux (1091–1153), *The Love of God, and Spiritual Friendship*, ed. James Houston, Multnomah Press (1983).

[2] Edward Shillito, *Jesus of the Scars* (1917).

THE GIFT OF BEING FULLY PRESENT

I am ashamed to admit it, but I am that guy who, when out for a meal in a pub, chooses the seat that will allow him to keep one eye on the football – which is deeply irritating to my family. We live in a culture stricken by a 'poverty-of-attention' disease and it desperately needs a cure. We've all been there: talking to someone who is not listening but rather planning what they are going to say next, speaking to a friend whose eyes are dancing around in search of someone more 'important'; trying to talk to a family member engrossed in their latest Facebook notification. Sometimes we can accept this deficit of attention as part of life, but we can feel a little less validated, a little less valued, a little less loved.

One of the most precious gifts you can give to another person is your time, and all your attention, so they know you are fully present and they have been heard. This kind of self-giving listening creates a safe place for vulnerability and trust, it allows pain and confusion to be articulated. I came to appreciate this gift in some of my friends but, more significantly, I came to understand it as an often unrecognized and immensely underrated characteristic of God.

I had made the choice to embrace the pain swirling around in my heart. I was prepared to stare into the heart of my darkness. I had mustered the courage to protest my disappointment before him. Now, I needed to know somehow, that he *heard* me, that I had been fully heard. Walking through the darkest part of the tunnel of grief I came to a new understanding of God – of his nature, of his kindness. I found God meeting me there and revealing to me the most beautiful paradox – that he was with me, profoundly with me. He was wholly present, utterly available and listening attentively.

Let me try to explain this next stage of discovery.

'GOD IS IN CONTROL'

Through these darkest of days, I learned that the most common line Christians use to bring comfort is 'God is in control' or 'don't worry, God still knows what he is doing'. I began to wonder if this was simply the *easiest* thing to say. At times there also seemed to be a moral and religious obligation to press this point home. In the weeks after Lindsay's death, I would bump into people who had heard the news of Lindsay's passing. With genuine sympathy many sought to encourage me, but they would simply say something like 'it's good we know God is in control, Alain'. These responses weren't wrong, of course, but I would walk away feeling frustrated. While appreciating their sincerity, I also couldn't deny the annoyance rising up inside me. I am acutely aware that I too have tried to console people in this way, in awkward moments, when I had nothing else to offer. 'God is in control, brother/sister.' What was it that bothered me about this?

I came to realize that this seems to be the Christian's default perspective on God's relationship to our suffering. And it inevitably leads to the impression of an impassive God, removed from our pain as he observes, righteous and remote, from heaven. But, don't worry, at least he is in control! A caricature, perhaps, but one that disturbed me.

I soon came to believe these platitudes are a smokescreen for repressed questions and doubts, that this response from 'comforters' (sometimes not unlike Job's comforters) is a frightened response, an indication of the need to avoid and explain away the darkness, from a safe vantage point, removed from the terrible reality the bereaved is experiencing. I saw that this is a protective mechanism, something to help us avoid exposing the real questions, doubt and pain buried in our hearts. 'At least God is in control' is a half-hearted attempt to engage with suffering, a response that gets comforters off the hook, and allows sufferers to avoid going to the heart of what we are *really* feeling and processing. As a result, we prevent God from going there with us, or rather from going where he is to be found, faced and deeply encountered. My experience of walking through acute pain revealed to me the gap there is in much of the church around the world today: we rush to *the God who is in control,* and give no time to *the God who suffers with us,* the One who meets us in our disappointment and joins with us in our mourning.

Blaise Pascal said, 'God made man in his own image and man returned the compliment'.[3] I would argue that this is never more true than when it comes to suffering. We will embrace a God who is in control simply because we want to feel that *we are still in control.* We embrace anything that reinforces our sense of safety, amid the turbulent swings of emotion in our tumultuous ever-changing world of loss, rather than risk the uncertainty of what it might mean to be truly honest about the questions assaulting our inner thoughts. Jonathan Martin[4] rightly concludes that experience of suffering often 'reinforces our masochistic views of God's sovereignty, damaging our fragile hearts in an attempt to find some kind of order or rationale in our heads'.

Stick with me …

I needed much more than platitudes, more than a flat theory of 'God is in control'. Dare I say it, but at this particular point in my journey of grief I needed something more. I searched scripture, I searched theologians and writers I respected: Brueggemann, Heschel, Wright and Moltmann, Yancey, Sittser and Wiman. A couple of months after Lindsay died, my friend Pete Greig came to visit, and as we were driving around he noticed a copy of Elie Wiesel's *Night* in the car. 'Alain', he said, 'what are you doing reading *this,* just at this point in your life?' I told him I just needed to read someone who had known the darkness I was experiencing in this moment. Then he got it and I felt reassured that it was ok to be ill at ease for a while. I just needed to engage with this.

The doctrine of impassibility is the belief that God is not subject to suffering, pain and the flow of involuntary passions and emotional reactions. Advocates of this doctrine argue that since God is unchanging in nature, his inner emotional state cannot change in the way human

---

[3] Blaise Pascal, source unknown.
[4] Jonathan Martin, via Twitter, https://twitter.com/theboyonthebike.

emotions do.[5] It is important to strive for a healthy tension. Let me try to explain.

Yes, God is in control. The fall of humanity and the disappointments of life don't threaten his overall control of things. He tells us, through the prophet Isaiah: 'I form light and create darkness, I make well-being and create calamity, I am the LORD, who does all these things' (Isaiah 45:7). Amid disaster and loss Job declares: 'In his hand is the life of every living thing and the breath of all mankind' (Job 12:10). Jesus himself says: 'Are not two sparrows sold for a penny? And not one of them will fall to the ground apart from your Father' (Matthew 10:29). God still has, as we were taught to sing in Sunday school, 'got the whole world in his hands'. It is true, and it is reassuring. When we are clueless and messed up, it's reassuring to know that God is not!

But when life falls apart, the logical but devastating conclusion of a tight-fisted doctrine of impassibility is that God is either distant and unconcerned with our lives, or more a remote deity than a loving Father. Knowing that God is in control may bring a measure of theoretical security, but it doesn't heal our broken hearts.

Scripture tells us that 'God is love' (1 John 4:8); that he is 'abounding in steadfast love and faithfulness, keeping steadfast love for thousands' (Exodus 34:6–7). It's one thing to affirm God's being in control, his sovereignty, characterized by steadfast, unfailing and all-encompassing love when life is good. But when your life collapses around you, how can you reconcile the two? How can you make any sense of it at all?

As I dared to voice my disappointment, as I leaned into my pain and let it fall before the face of God, I also saw that I needed to allow a true understanding of the nature of God to shape my pain, and not let my

---

[5] To be fair, not all theologians who hold to the doctrine of impassibility say that God is completely indifferent to human emotions – some argue more accurately the emphasis lies in the voluntary nature of God's reaction to his creation.

pain shape my image of God. Somehow, as I wrestled, I began to see that our understanding of God's control must not be held in isolation from our understanding of other significant truths about God.

For as long as I can remember, I have known that Jesus died for me on the cross, that he had suffered brutally and cruelly for me (and the whole world), that he rose from the dead, and if I trusted in his redemptive work it would save my soul. There would be peace with God in this age and eternal security in heaven with him when I died. This was good news, but I hadn't grasped the profound implications that this had for me *in the present.* I was thankful Jesus had gone to these unfathomable self-sacrificial lengths for my soul in the name of love, but I was unaware of the beauty of *what this could mean for me now.* I knew God had suffered *for* me but I had never really understood that he suffered *with* me. I had been content that a theological transaction had taken place at the cross securing my eternal security without ever understanding that Jesus' cross-shaped love was also a revelation to humanity of the *co-suffering* nature of God. This revelation came in the silent, alone moments when I became aware, despite my frustration with God that he was present – weeping with me, helping me grieve.

More tangibly this truth was incarnated through my dad during those unbearable nights when I was back in my parents' house. The nights when a wave of grief would come, the ache so deep and searing that it could express itself only in loud groans. On these nights, my dad would come into my room and just sit there, on the edge of my bed. He would sit quietly in the dark but I could hear him weep with me. He never said anything in those moments except once, and I can still remember his tender voice, 'Alain, if I could take this for you, son, I would take it all now, if the Lord would let me, I would take it for you.'

Through these darkest of days, I became aware through the gentle presence of God and the example of my dad of this glorious and fuller truth. The incarnation, culminating in Jesus' death and resurrection means *God suffers not just for me but with me.* He is deeply entwined in my *present* pain and the brokenness of the world he loves.

OLD TESTAMENT WITNESS TO THE PATHOS OF GOD

As I began to pay careful attention to the scriptures, as I wrestled with the theology, I began to see not an angry tyrant or a remote deity, but a grieving parent. I began to discover a paradigm for the co-suffering nature of God. I began to see that God does not rule simply by control, He rules by love. There is a difference. Father God's anger originates out of his love. He is still in control, and the overarching narrative reveals that, despite mankind's failures, God's promises and plans still hold true.

Growing up, I had seen the anger, vengeance and punishment of God in parts of the Bible, and in my worst times had seen God as a cosmic kill-joy or an aggressive control freak. I found Walter Brueggemann's reflections on the flood narrative (Genesis 6) particularly helpful in exposing my twisted perceptions.

Brueggemann shows how the opening pages of scripture describe an engaging, inviting Father God, who is grieved, troubled, broken-hearted by the decisions his creation have made. In Genesis 6:6, 'And the LORD regretted that he had made man on the earth, and it grieved him to his heart', the word used for 'grieve' is the same word used for 'pain' in Genesis 3:16, describing pain in childbirth for Eve.[6] For a woman at the height of labour the pain is overwhelming, eclipsing all else, causing even the most timid to roar and cry out. This primal, physical image is the one used to describe the deep anguish in the Father's heart when humanity rejects his loving and glorious designs for their lives. Colourless, technical language cannot begin to describe God's interaction with his creation. Instead, scripture uses the passionate, intimate, physical language of childbirth, and of lovers. God *feels* the pain of his image bearers. The essence of the Biblical story is God entering fully into that pain so he can establish the trust and obedience that he is inviting his creation into:

---

[6] Walter Brueggemann, *Interpretation: A Bible Commentary for Teaching and Preaching*, Westminster John Knox Press, 1st edition (25 January 2010).

The daring assertion about God is problematic in every static theology which wants God always acting the same and predictably. But the text affirms that God is decisively impacted by the suffering, hurt and circumstances of his creation. God entered into the world's 'common lot'.[7]

As I read on through the Old Testament I began to see that from the beginning, God's will was not so much coercive and dictatorial but rather invitational and gracious; that his rule came often through astonishing displays of vulnerability.

While we try to find ways to protect ourselves, to keep ourselves from being vulnerable, God unzips his heart to humanity. God is the Father of creation who opens his heart to us. He reveals the sheer delight he has in his image-bearers coming to know him in covenant relationships and the heartbreak he suffers over his oppressed and wayward children. He is the God that stands outside of time yet the God who is closer than our next breath, wading through the muck and mire of a broken humanity to meet us in the middle of our mess. He is never presented in scripture as a God who is aloof, insulated from our sufferings. I saw this most vividly in God's response to the plight of the Hebrew slaves, tyrannized under Pharaoh's brutal Egyptian regime:

> Then the LORD said, "I have *observed* the misery of my people who are in Egypt; I have *heard* their cry on account of their taskmasters. Indeed, I *know* their sufferings, and I have *come down* to deliver them from the Egyptians, and to *bring* them up out of that land to a good and broad land, a land flowing with milk and honey, to the country of the Canaanites, the Hittites, the Amorites, the Perizzites, the Hivites, and the Jebusites. The cry of the Israelites has now come to me; I have also seen how the Egyptians oppress them.
>
> Exodus 3:7–9 NRSV (italics mine)

---

[7] Walter Brueggemann, *Interpretation: A Bible Commentary for Teaching and Preaching*.

God *observes* our misery – he sees it.
God *hears* our cries.
God *knows* our sufferings.
God *comes down* to deliver.
God *brings us into* a new place.

I read the great Jewish theologian, Abraham Heschel, who introduced me to the concept of 'the divine pathos' – the title of this chapter and the word that encapsulates all I am seeking to convey in these pages. Heschel refutes any notion of God as a commander of mankind, demanding obedience, impersonal and aloof, unaffected by the pain and circumstances of human beings. He contends that, in his omnipotence, grandeur and perfection, he is a God of feeling and *pathos* – intimately and emotionally connected to humankind, a God who is deeply concerned and engaged in the affairs of those created in his image. God does not simply 'feel sorry for you' – he is 'cognizant with our most inward emotions', his heart interwoven with ours through our gravest agonies. God has *always* been trying to communicate this to us. Heschel argues in his seminal work *The Prophets* how through the lives and words of the Old Testament prophets we become aware of 'a communion with the divine consciousness' – the divine pathos. Hosea and Jeremiah acted out the pain felt by God using intimate and costly metaphors. Hosea is called to marry a whore and forgive her unfaithfulness time after time, Jeremiah to break a flask, to buy a field during a siege, to be cast into a cistern. I read the words of their contemporary, Isaiah: 'In all their affliction he was afflicted' (Isaiah 63:9) and I realize the pathos of God reveals *both* his wounded and wonderful nature.

Get this ... our pain is *his* pain.

Where I used to see only the wrath of God, I now see windows into the intense suffering of God. He is the God of the weathered face and he is found amongst the poor, the sick, the dying and those left to mourn. I began to form a picture of an outrageously merciful and compassionate God whose *almighty power is matched by* his *almighty love*, the King of the Universe who makes his home among the broken and punctured of heart.

Pathos revealed in Jesus

This God, I was beginning to see in my reading of the Old Testament, deeply impacted by the pain and rebellion of his people, eventually enters into the world's common lot as the incarnate Lord and ultimately absorbs the pain of the world into his own personal being. Philip Kenneson summarizes the clear message of God's suffering love throughout the whole of scripture: 'the incarnation represents not a change in plans but the supreme expression of the lengths to which God is willing to go in order to embody this eternal, steadfast, suffering love.'[8] I learned through my luminous darkness that God is *so* sovereign, he chooses to save the world by allowing himself to become *power-less* (in human terms). Jesus shows us the face and the heart of God and reveals to us that the most powerful act in history is the most self-giving and sacrificial act in history. 'When God wants to flex his omnipotent muscle', Greg Boyd says, 'it looks like a cross'.[9]

I always knew that one of the titles associated with the Son of God is the *Suffering Servant*, that this was prophesied in the Jewish scriptures, most explicitly through Isaiah, and first-century Jews would have been schooled in the sacred promises that the Saviour of the world would be associated with suffering. I was aware of how the 'Creator of the ends of the earth' (Isaiah 40:28) would be 'a man of sorrows and acquainted with grief' (Isaiah 53:3), and how Jesus knew he was born for this hour (John 12:27), knowing his long walk of obedience would reveal the essence of the good news of the kingdom he came pronouncing – life comes through death. For me, it was now more than a theory or an object lesson. I began to see it as a real-life demonstration of love as Jesus shows, in the fullness of his humanity, the 'death-leading-to-life' kind of life.

I am a firm believer in the Lordship and divinity of Christ. However, I am equally astounded by the Son of God's humanity. The

---

[8] Philip D. Kenneson, *Life on the Vine: Cultivating the Fruit of the Spirit in Christian Community*, InterVarsity Press (1999).
[9] I came across this insight listening to a Greg Boyd sermon in his church, Woodland Hills.

vulnerability of God, revealed in Christ, is stupefying. We need not be so nervous about this in the church. For too long Jesus has been too stained-glassed, exposing an underwhelming understanding of his humanity. Jesus does not only show us what divinity looks like, he shows us what humanity in its fullest and truest form looks like. He was 'tempted in every way, just as we are – yet he did not sin' (Hebrews 4:15 NIV). He teaches us how to become a God-like image-bearer and a follower of his way. In doing so he shows us how to be fully human. This is the one who wept at the death of his friend, celebrated with his friends at a wedding, asked for a drink at a well, enjoyed nick-naming his mates, worked alongside his dad in the family business, experienced the full range of human emotions that we do and ultimately when his side was pierced on Calvary spilled out blood and water. 'Since the children have flesh and blood, he too shared in their humanity' (Hebrews 2:14 NIV). Embracing the humanity of Jesus does not need to make us nervous. On the contrary, it should fill us with ever-expanding wonder of his magnificence and appreciation for the gift and liberty it offers us.

In contemplating the humanity of Jesus, I am drawn deeper into the person of Jesus, startled and in awe of how he endured for humanity, how he was deserted on several occasions by his closest friends, ridiculed by the masses, misunderstood and falsely accused. How at 33 (the age I am as I write this) he carried the hopes and destinies of the human race on his shoulders.

> He was despised and rejected by mankind,
> a man of suffering, and familiar with pain.
>
> Isaiah 53:3 NIV

Yes, God is in control. That is crucial for our existence, never mind our salvation, but most of us reading this book don't need that sermon preached at us right now. Rather, we need to grasp the implications of the incarnation and to encounter Jesus as our *Wounded Healer* – a God who *enters into* our suffering. We know he suffered *for* us, at Calvary all those years ago, but we need to know that because of this, he suffers *with us* today, in our darkest hours.

> Surely he took up our pain
> and bore our suffering.
>
> Isaiah 53:4 NIV

I came to discover as I walked through the darkest parts of my valley of the shadow of death the liberating and glorious centerpiece of scriptural truth: that God meets us in our most hopeless state. He doesn't just ask us to give him our best – he asks us to bring him our worst. He is more than worthy of the best we can give him, but it's also the worst of us that he is after, and where he wants to reveal his goodness. Our ugliest sin, our greatest heartache, our deepest grief, our violent rage. Not only did he ultimately bear it in his own body to pave a victorious path of freedom for us, but his journey towards this sacrificial death reveals how in his humanity he carried pain of monumental proportions. The gospel writers give us glimpses into Jesus' humanity during his final hours, and in doing so reveal to us how we can journey through our own dark days of apparent forsakenness. They tell us of anguish so severe that his sweat was like drops of blood on the ground. How did Jesus deal with this inconceivable level of anguish? Again, he prayed it: 'Father, is there any other way? Nevertheless, not my will but yours be done.'[10] The emotional anguish Jesus was carrying in the garden became an even harder experience of deep emotional forsakenness when he hung on the cross. The harrowing cry from Golgotha of, 'my God, my God why have you forsaken me?' stands alone as the starkest in all of scripture. Any further permission we need, as regards protesting our pain, we find here in the hours when darkness covered the whole earth. In excruciating physical pain of a brutal crucifixion, coupled with the torment of 'becoming sin' for the entire human race, Jesus cried the most powerful lament ever uttered. What did Jesus do with this extreme sense of forsakenness? Again, he prayed it. We have permission to voice before the Father the most agonizing shrieks of our soul. Jesus never denied the pain, the grief, the heartache, the loneliness or his genuine experience of the presence of the Holy as forsakenness. He cried it out in prayer. The Son of God yelled out his

---

[10] John 12: my paraphrase.

incomprehensible pain, from the depths of him to the Father who he felt had abandoned him. For a fraction of time this *was* death with a sting and darkness without light. Heaven was silent and the Father wept. Jesus prayed out the torment and impending loss, as Macleod notes in *The Person of Christ*:

> As he hangs on the cross, bleeding, battered, powerless and forsaken the last thing he looks like is God. Indeed, he scarcely looks human.[11]

We cannot overestimate the depth of desolation of these words of forsakenness. A great deal of our faith and theology hang on a proper understanding of them, and they were of particular help to me through my own lonely and dark nights. Christian Wiman describes his own valley of the shadow of death and, profoundly, the importance of Jesus' 'God-forsaken' prayer as the bedrock of his faith:

> I am a Christian because of that moment on the cross when Jesus, drinking the very dregs of human bitterness, cries out, 'My God, My God why have you forsaken me.' … the point is that he felt human destitution to its absolute degree; the point is God is with us not beyond us in suffering. I am a Christian because I understand that moment of Christ's passion to have meaning in my own life and what it means is that the absolute solitary and singular nature of extreme human pain is an illusion. I'm not suggesting that ministering angels are going to come and minister to you as you die. I'm suggesting that Christ's suffering shatters the iron walls around individual human suffering, that Christ's compassion makes extreme human compassion – to the point of death even – possible.[12]

The implications of this should bring immense comfort – God is *present* in your suffering. The unquantifiable and indescribable level of his pain means he is more than qualified to understand and enter into yours, when no one else can. His experience of no 'WITHNESS' means

---

[11] Donald Macleod, *The Person of Christ (Contours of Christian Theology)*, InterVarsity Press Academic, unknown edition (6 December 1998).
[12] Christian Wiman, *My Bright Abyss: Meditation of a Modern Believer*, Farrar, Straus Giroux, reprint edition (April 2014).

wherever you are he can be WITH you. He was the first to cry when your loved one died, the first to weep when your partner walked out on you, the first to feel your pain when you received that tragic news. Because of the cross of Jesus, 'the singular nature of extreme human pain is an illusion'.[13] You are not alone. He is there. He is not like me, half-listening, sort of attentive, watching the football, partly present. He is FULLY PRESENT and there is not a tear he does not notice.

> You have kept count of my tossings;
> put my tears in your bottle.
> Are they not in your book?
>
> Psalm 56:8

Jürgen Moltmann, in his seminal work, *The Crucified God*, summarized here by Greg Boyd, has in particular emphasized that:

> only by affirming the authenticity of Jesus' God-forsakenness can we affirm that God has fully entered into, fully experienced, fully embraced and fully redeemed the God-forsakenness of the world. Because the Son experienced the horror of God-forsakenness, and because the Father experienced the horror of forsaking his Son, we can affirm that 'even Auschwitz is taken up into the grief of the Father, the surrender of the Son and the power of the Spirit.' In the nightmarish separation of the Father and Son, he writes, we can see that 'the whole uproar of history,' with all of its unthinkable atrocities, is embraced 'within God.'[14]

The Godhead was *never more* involved than in the death of the Son. During that holy separation, the three divine persons of the Trinity were willing to sacrifice their previously perfect and uninterrupted unity in order to reveal the very nature of who they are. As Paul said: 'God was **in Christ** reconciling the world to himself.' This is what they had planned from the foundation of the world. Jesus wasn't so much saving us from the Father as he was revealing the heart of the

---

[13] Christian Wiman, *My Bright Abyss: Meditation of a Modern Believer.*
[14] Greg Boyd, http://reknew.org/2013/05/when-god-abandoned-god/.

Father to us. Yes, for the greater joy ahead, the Father didn't intervene, but he was *there* and because of this, he is *always there. God is always there.* Jesus reveals to us exactly what God looks like and on the cross Jesus demonstrates what God is prepared to go through to rescue and restore every broken part of us.

To our minds this is foolishness, but St Paul's great refrain meets this head on: 'the foolishness of God is wiser than men, and the weakness of God is stronger than men.' God's greatest act of sovereignty is expressed through the most astounding act of vulnerability the world has ever seen.

My God is not insecure. His love rules and endures through pain.

Darkness is his secret place

All these readings, reflections and discoveries around God meeting me in my pain formed a reference point and a place from which I felt I could *truly* pray. They are summarized in the scripture given to me by my mum, who prayed for me unceasingly in those days. Like my dad, she wished she could do more, she longed to rescue me from this tragedy, but she found a measure of peace in a verse in Psalm 18 and after she offered it to me I prayed it aloud over and over again.

> He made darkness his secret place;
> his pavilion round about him
> were dark waters and thick clouds of the skies.
>
> Psalm 18:11 KJV

The part of me no one else could get to, my own secret pain which no one else could fully understand, God made his 'secret place'. In Jesus, God has been to the grave and back. As the Psalmist reminds us when we make our bed there (Psalm 139:8) even then he will find us and come to us. In Jesus, God has been lower than all of us and so he alone is the only one who can fully meet us in that place. Not just because he is God and he can do everything in a theoretical and technical kind of way that fudges the reality of our pain and forsakenness but because he *actually experienced* it. He *felt* it. On the cross he embodied our pain. He gathered up the pain of the world and took it *into* himself. God has been to deeper levels of pain than any of us and is therefore 'qualified' to meet us in our deepest ache. Cornelius Plantinga Jr articulates this wonderfully:

> We do not refer each other to the cross of Christ to explain evil. It is not as if in pondering Calvary we will at last understand throat cancer. We rather lift up our eyes to the cross, whence comes our help, in order to see that God shares our lot and can therefore be trusted.[15]

Often we can emphasize God's 'otherness' at the expense of his nearness. We perceive God as absent more than as radically present. We are used to looking at the empty cross all year, and for good reason, such is the magnificence of the resurrection and its implications for salvation and restoration. Yet I wonder do we miss something by not developing a more sacramental imagination – where we are content to simply sit at the dying Saviour's feet, entering into his death, allow him to enter into ours and wait until we hear the monumental words 'it is finished'? After all, resurrection can be enjoyed only when death has been tasted. It is the worst of me that needs to hear 'it is finished', it is my deepest grief and pain that needs to hear 'it is finished' before I can even begin to contemplate the reality of complete restoration and wholeness. I need to hear 'it is finished' before a new beginning can truly begin to take place.

A different type of fixing

It doesn't help that we are obsessed with fixing things. Peterson says with candour: 'suffering attracts fixers the way a roadkill attracts vultures.'[16] He is not far wrong. Our words are an attempt to fill a silence that can't be filled with words and therefore offer only a false sense of security. We are not machines that need to be fixed. We are humans who need

---

[15] Cornelius Plantinga, Jr, 'A love so fierce', *The Reformed Journal* (November 1986).
[16] Eugene H. Peterson, *The Message: The Bible in Contemporary Language.*

connection. We can't get out of our suffering through our heads, only through our hearts. I am glad that God is in control; I knew he could handle what was going on when it felt like the walls were caving in around me. Yet in the darkest day of my pain it wasn't primarily what I needed to hear. I hadn't doubted that God was in control: it was just that in the reality of those unbearable early days I needed to know that God was *with* me, that he hadn't forgotten me and that he was *fully present* with me.

He had made my darkness his secret place. My prayer of lament was given as much of a hearing in heaven as my prayer of celebration. My personal prayer of pain found a place of reference in the most powerful act in history.

Don't let pain shape your image of God; let your image of God shape your pain.

Only a proper understanding of this will help us break up the hard-crusted earth covering our unspoken agonies, pour in healing rain and prepare us for the seeds of new life and hope-filled possibility. But let's not get ahead of ourselves – there were more things to learn in the darkest parts of this slow and painstaking journey through grief. In particular, I was coming to understand the deafening and disorientating silence of Holy Saturday.

CHAPTER SIX

SILENCE

Can you see how our very sense of the absence of God is, therefore, an unsuspected grace? It is in the very act of hiddenness God is slowly weaning us from fashioning him in our own image.[1]

Richard Foster

Before the gospel is a word, it is silence.[2]

Frederick Buechner

Silence is a strange, mysterious wonder. There are times when silence can be distinctly uncomfortable, like when nervous young lovers on a first date try to fill gaps in conversation; or when a teacher asks a simple question but is met with vacant stares. There are times when silence can be warm and reassuring, as when two old friends sit for hours together without needing to talk; or when the crazy house settles down after the kids have gone to bed and you relax in your favourite chair with a glass of wine; or when you walk along a quiet country road at dusk. While sometimes unsettling, particularly for the

---

[1] Richard Foster, *Prayer: Finding the Heart's True Home.*
[2] Frederick Buechner, *Listening to Your Life: Daily Meditations with Frederick Buechner,* HarperCollins (1992).

extrovert, silence makes space for rest and reflection, and can become a means to deeper connection and higher learning.

The experience of silence is something the church fathers, and mystics down through church history, have much to teach us about. Thomas Aquinas and Martin Luther are two theological heavyweights who articulated *Deus Absconditus*, the God who is hidden, drawn from Isaiah 45:15. Living through seasons when God is on mute[3] seems to be a spiritual prerequisite for any journey into the deeper recesses of the heart of God. Before my experience of loss, I had read about this season in classics of the Christian faith, and viewed it as something slightly esoteric, but also just a step of spiritual growth up the discipleship ladder, which I presumed I could navigate relatively easily. I had romanticized the contemplative side of these silent days, underestimating what it would involve, and the part of me that enjoyed my own company looked forward to the solitary nature of such an experience.

I was in for a shock. The days of living and processing my grief brought a stark and tormenting reality check. I learned what the silent and dark night of the soul is really like.

MADDENING SILENCE

I had no idea how maddening and debilitating the days of silence would be. Equally I had no idea how life-changing it would be. What do you do when you cry out to God but hear nothing back? How do you deal with the frustration of being desperate for answers, yelling out questions but getting no reply? How do you live through a storm while all the time Jesus is sleeping in the boat? C.S. Lewis describes the infuriation that rises in the distressed heart searching frantically for answers: 'Knock and it shall be opened. But does knocking mean hammering and kicking the door like a maniac?'[4]

---

[3] This expression comes from the title of Pete Greig's book, *God on Mute: Engaging the Silence of Unanswered Prayer.*

[4] C.S. Lewis, *A Grief Observed.*

I had protested, and that brought catharsis to my soul. I had come to realize God suffered *with* me, and that brought deep comfort. But there was still a constant, and at times uncontrollable, impatience, demanding reasons and answers, explanations to fill the nothingness, a passionate inquisition of God:

Why?
What on earth next?
Who have I become?
What do I do?
Who am I becoming?

I had lived through my own Gethsemane, surrendering my heart to God's sovereign goodness in Lindsay's final days. I had experienced something of the agony of Good Friday – something of the death and apparent forsakenness by God. Now it appeared I had passed into Holy Saturday, living through my own paschal mystery, a space characterized by nothingness. Elusive, vague, nebulous silence.

Waiting. Silence.
Questions. Silence.
More questions. Silence.

'Wake up God, wake up from your sleep!'

Silence.

In my worst moments, frustration spilled over into petulant outbursts, and the desperation for answers was so fierce it felt like a fire raging inside me. I feared that fire might burn me up, and it scorched all who allowed me to vent in their presence. I wasn't getting answers and it was driving me insane. The words of Andrew Peterson's haunting song 'The Silence of God' resonated deeply:

It's enough to drive a man crazy; it'll break a man's faith
It's enough to make him wonder if he's ever been sane

When he's bleating for comfort from Thy staff and Thy rod
And the heaven's only answer is the silence of God.[5]

I continued to wrestle with God, but we wrestled now largely in silence.
I thought I deserved explanations, but came to realize I wasn't going
to get any. The truth is: silence does not mean absence. God inhabits
silence. Mystery himself is found in the secret and silent desert space.

> Be still, and know that I am God.
>
> Psalm 46:10

PRESENCE AND SILENCE

The implication of Presence (God's presence or 'with-ness') revealed
through Scripture is that something, or someone, is being experienced
beyond what words can describe. God *IS* presence – sheer being,
which means his essence is a way of being. We are encountered in ways
much deeper than language could ever articulate or explain. More
than obtaining my rights as in a normal earthbound legal contract,
I was bound in a richer covenant-relationship with the triune God,
expressed through a giving up of my rights and a rugged commitment
of sacrificial love. Faith, I was learning, is not an intellectual assent
but a commitment to a covenant partner. In the silence, I learned
that a much deeper communion is experienced which is impossible
to grasp unless you have gone through the undoing of those God-
on-mute days. None of your questions get answered. At worst, it feels
like they are being ignored, yet you are suspended in a looming sense
of presence that moves beyond mere feeling to deeper levels of soul-
consciousness. This sense of presence transcends cognitive abilities
and descends to a more primal part of our beings. I wouldn't call it
comforting or even encouraging, but I could say there is an unusual
reassurance in it.

---

[5] Andrew Peterson, 'The Silence of God', Provident Label Group LLC, a unit of Sony
BMG Music Entertainment (2003).

This was my blog entry in the days I engaged in the silence of God:

I cannot see his plan but I am trying to trust in his heart His heart that is good, that is love and mercy. His heart that is for us. It is a hard thing to do – trust in his heart when you don't know his plan; when you can't hear his voice; when your cries and groans seem to fill the empty air all around; when you plead for comfort but heaven's only answer is the silence of God. I believe he is here, wounded and grieving with me, broken and bruised, but I want more. I want him to fix it – to give her back. In times like these we opt for the 'God is in control' answer in order to put to bed all our questions. For me, though, I have found God to be a God who appears to relinquish control in these times. The God who can fix things – doesn't. At least not the way we would like him to. The God who loves us more than we know chooses not to intervene the way we would like him to. This is the hardest place to be with God. Like on that Friday when Jesus was being crucified and hung on a cross bearing the sin of the whole world. God could have done something, but he didn't. He had to watch. We can't even imagine the pain and anguish but he chose to watch because he saw something else. Something bigger. Something better. Jesus, who for the joy set before him endured the cross. The pain then is part of the joy now. He saw beyond the cross, beyond Friday – he saw the Sunday, the resurrection. And the joy was that he saw you and me today with the life of Christ in us, all because of that terrible/good Friday. I only know in part. I only see through a glass dimly. You are God and not man, Hosea proclaimed. He must see things we don't. I can't see the Sunday yet, I don't know if I fully will in this life. But I have to believe in it because I am still in Friday/Saturday and all I can hear is the silence of God. And it would be impossible to stay here for too long. So I try to trust in the God of Love who sees stuff I don't.

Surrendering to silence is frightening. 'It is a fearful thing to fall into the hands of the living God' (Hebrews 10:31). It is about letting go of everything and falling into God, falling into mystery, what Richard Rohr describes as the 'Compassionate Abyss'. A kind of holy fear envelops our beings in this season of silence because, in letting go, it feels like the end for us. Yet the paradox in such a 'death' is in completely letting go of all our preconditions and preconceived ideas, the end becomes the beginning. There is something about the human heart that fully learns to trust God only when we have nothing else to lean on. Feeling dead in the silence, we fall into the arms of the loving God who is fully alive. Because God is not completely who we thought he was, we must wait for fresh revelation. We wait because we have a hunch that this Mystery knows us better than we know ourselves and is inviting us into a Love that calls our name.[6] There is no easy way other than to trust the process amid the silence. Accept what has happened. Relinquish control. Let go of the abstract mental images and philosophical reasoning. Fall into God. As Thomas Merton wrote: 'sometimes no explanation is sufficient to account for suffering. The only decent thing is silence, and the sacraments.'[7]

THE DIFFICULTY WITH SILENCE TODAY

Yet this is so difficult for us in our media-saturated world. We deal with trauma on a global level on our TVs, computer screens and smart-phones. Yet we fill the grief-torn spaces with words and, worse, with heinous explanations. Grappling with the aftermath of the Sandy Hook Elementary School shooting in 2012 where Adam Lanza shot dead twenty children and six adults, Andy Crouch powerfully observed that our responses leave no room for silence:

---

[6] These thoughts are inspired by a poem of Debbie Thomas, *Why I Stay: A Prayer.*
[7] Thomas Merton, source unknown.

someone must always be saying something even when there is nothing new to say … The grieving, the sick, and the dying some-times need our words, sometimes need our touch, but almost always they need our presence. And there is no contradiction between presence **and silence in the embodied life for which we were all created, to which we are all called, into which God himself entered.** Bodies can be present without a word. That is the beauty of bodies.[8] (**bold** mine)

'There is no contradiction between silence and presence …' Think about that for a moment. Think how counter-cultural that is.

Going on current cultural trends, #silence doesn't look like it is going to make it as a trending topic. Silence is never going to have much street credibility. We should discipline ourselves not to substitute 'information for contemplation, the illusion of engagement for prayer'.[9] Yes, prayer. This is the only place we can embrace the silence, where we learn to stay with God in the midst of pain, 'without answers, without conclusions and some days without meaning'. This has been called 'the perilous path of true prayer'.[10] Here, we learn that the primary place of connection with God in these turbulent days is not our head but our heart. My advice: allow your heart to override your head in these days. Be still and know he is God. Fully present, fully engaged. As we surrender to his will above our own, to his mystery above our rational wisdom, to his silence above our independent constructs, sometimes the secret things that belong to the Lord will be revealed to us. I came to realize that if we seek the answers we won't find them but if we seek God the answers will find us in due time.[11] When we fully embrace Mystery himself we often end up with revelations we would not otherwise have discovered. Jesus gives us reason to believe this counter-intuitive way of knowing is his desire for us:

---

[8] Andy Crouch, *Christianity Today: The Media and the Massacre. True compassion requires turning off the news* (19 December 2012).

[9] Andy Crouch, *Christianity Today: The Media and the Massacre. True compassion requires turning off the news.*

[10] Jonathan Martin, via Twitter, https://twitter.com/theboyonthebike.

[11] This is a paraphrase from Mark Batterson's book *The Circle Maker: Praying Circles Around Your Biggest Dreams and Greatest Fears*, Zondervan; reprint edition (18 December 2012).

> At that time Jesus declared, 'I thank you, Father, Lord of
> heaven and earth, that you have hidden these things from the
> wise and understanding and revealed them to little children.'
>
> Matthew 11:25

It pleases the Father to reveal his heart, the wisdom of heaven, to us through the Spirit. We should grasp this truth with both hands but temper it with a reminder from the apostle Paul, that his ways are 'past finding out!' (Romans 11:33 KJV). I came to learn that there were times I had to trust God more than understand him. He has reasons, in his infinitely pure and incomprehensible loving heart, our heads will never know. Yet, mysteriously and tremendously his immediate presence can fill up every hole that has been punctured in our hearts. The prayers that we pray when we hear nothing back leave us in a place where we must learn to fall out of our heads and into our hearts, trusting that all the time we are falling into him.

> All you can do is abide in God, and then God holds the tensions in you
> and through you and with you – and largely in spite of you.[12]

'WAKE UP, GOD'

As we sit in the 'silence of God' we should not do it resignedly. We should continue to lean into it. Leaning into the silence with accompanied stillness is, at times, all we can do, but our frustrations still need to be voiced. Like Job and the Psalmists, the indiscriminate prayers continue even when the heavens seem like brass (Deuteronomy 28:23 KJV).

> I shout for help, God, and get nothing, no answer!
> I stand to face you in protest, and you give me a blank stare!
> Job 30:20 MSG

---

[12] Richard Rohr, *Richard Rohr's Daily Meditation: Stable Witness* (Wednesday 30 July 2014).

though I call and cry for help,
he shuts out my prayer;
he has blocked my ways with blocks of stones;
he has made my paths crooked.

Lamentations 3:8–9

O my God, I cry by day, but you do not answer,
and by night, but I find no rest.

Psalm 22:2

Get up, GOD! Are you going to sleep all day?
Wake up! Don't you care what happens to us?
Why do you bury your face in the pillow?
Why pretend things are just fine with us?
And here we are – flat on our faces in the dirt,
held down with a boot on our necks.
Get up and come to our rescue.
If you love us so much, Help us!

Psalm 44:23–26 MSG

Much of these ancient texts stay in this place of prayer of crying out to God, of formulating prayers even when they are met by silence. These prayers point to the prayer of Jesus on the cross who, sensing himself utterly abandoned by God, still finds a way to ask God why he has abandoned him. We explored this prayer in detail in the previous chapter, but let's reflect some more on how it meets silence, more profound and mysterious than any other in history. The cry 'Why?' from Jesus provoked no spoken response from the Father. Silence. Darkness. A question. Emptiness. Nothing. Silence. He cried out in his moment of greatest need and appeared not to be heard. I have described in the previous chapter how the humanity of Jesus expressed in this anguished cry connected with my soul in a way that helped assure me God *knew* my pain. Now I was experiencing even deeper resonance as I began to meditate on the mystery of an apparent juxtaposition: Jesus' agonizing, forsaken prayer was met with silence from his Father, yet Jesus, as he prayed, was unquestionably in the centre of the Godhead's plan for humanity, a plan designed before the foundation of the world. A plan that took into account humanity's rebellion, the de-creation of God's good world which broke his heart and the rescue that was foreordained through the incarnation of Jesus. This mystery brought me consolation and some security, and my confidence began to grow. Jesus set an example by going through pain and darkness of an incomparable nature, while experiencing the silence of the Father, yet still right in the centre of the plan of God. It empowered me to contemplate that the silence I was experiencing did not mean I was 'outside' of God's plan. In fact, because my prayer in life had been for God to 'break my heart for what breaks his', maybe I was where God wanted me. I had no explanations, maybe I simply needed to wait – let God be God in the midst of the silence. Peterson's words mentored me in those days: 'waiting in prayer is a disciplined refusal to act before God acts'.[13]

I made a promise to God – I was never going to stand up and give him glory for my healing until I knew I was truly healed, until I knew I had met him in the Sahara of my heart. To be honest, the reoccurring whisper, 'Alain, be true to your pain', gave me encouragement to steady my heart through these silent days and not to rush out of them. The silence became the place where I let go of my 'self' and tried my best

---

[13] Eugene Peterson, via Twitter, https://twitter.com/PetersonDaily.

to rest in 'the Big Self, in the God Self, in the One who knows all, loves all, and holds all things in their seeming imperfection'.[14] My favourite verses of scripture in this season were the exquisitely inspired words of the apostle Paul 'You have died and your life is hidden with Christ in God' (Colossians 3:3). I had lived through my own Friday and now I was sitting/resting in the silence of Saturday – and that was ok because God lived through Saturday too.

I think I was concerned I would have only a superficial Sunday experience if I didn't allow myself to fully embrace Saturday. It wasn't that I enjoyed Saturday, but intuitively I knew I couldn't let myself settle for a rushed and unfinished, disingenuous processing of my grief. I couldn't patronize the pain. I had an inner conviction that living through Saturday was no less spiritual and no less holy than a forced Easter Sunday experience would be. Sometimes we just have to wait it out and know him in the silence, know him in our own living hell. Anne Lamott surmises: 'to heal we have to stand in the middle of the horror at the foot of the cross and wait out another suffering where that person can see us.'[15]

PRAYERFUL SILENCE

In retrospect, silence was the only adequate response to my darkest days; the only way of ensuring my pain wasn't belittled or mis-understood. I didn't like it at the time but I have come to learn that silence is sometimes the most appropriate response to anguish and pain. I stumbled my way into a renewed understanding of the importance of contemplative prayer in these seasons. Waiting in prayer. Waiting, not in a resigned way, but engaging my heart with the process of transformation going on within me. The Bible refers to this kind of waiting as patient endurance (Romans 5:4; Hebrews 10:36; James 5:10-11; Revelation 2:2, 19). It is not a mild and benign acceptance, the kind

---

[14] Richard Rohr, *Richard Rohr's Daily Meditation: Stable Witness* (Wednesday 30 July 2014).

[15] Anne Lamott, *Stitches: A Handbook on Meaning, Hope and Repair.*

of boring process associated with the waiting room of the doctor's surgery. Rather it is a dogged determination, more akin to a marathon runner, carrying excruciating pain in their body, longing for the finish line, yet stubborn in their desire to complete the course.

This kind of contemplative prayer drew me slowly deeper into myself and into God, enabling me to see a higher way and a broader horizon than my dualistic mindset had allowed for. My worldview had been, I was learning, simplistic and reductionist. Of the information, circumstances and experiences that found their way to me, I had been taking in and processing only the pieces I liked, only the parts that supported my personal outlook. This, though, is only half of life. In the silence of God I was forced to hold the other half of life – the dark and broken side – before his face, and in doing so I was bringing *all of life* to God in prayer. God is Mystery and only in embracing the mystery of all of life could I fully embrace God himself. I was only seeing through a glass darkly. In these days of silence I had to put away childish thinking. I had to think like a man, and to think like a man meant embracing mystery and wrapping my arms around silence in a loving embrace. Counterintuitively I had to learn that independent certainty would kill the romance of relationship with God. In the words of John O'Donohue, I discovered 'the secret and the sacred are sisters. When the secret is not respected the sacred vanishes.'[16] Faith and wholehearted trust in the mystery was where love himself was to be found and a knowledge far beyond mere reason. Heschel sums it up so well: 'The search for reason ends at the shore of the known, on the immense expanse beyond it only the sense of ineffable can glide.'[17]

The Psalms are masterly expressions of contemplative and waiting prayer. Active waiting. Patient waiting. Persistent waiting. Psalm 139 speaks poetically of our inability to escape God. This Psalm is often quoted to remind us that God is with us in all our daily activities, wherever we find ourselves. Another layer of truth is that even when

[16] John O'Donohue, *Anam Cara*, Bantam, new edition (1 April 1999).
[17] Abraham Joshua Heschel, *Man Is Not Alone: A Philosophy of Religion*, Farrar, Straus and Giroux, reissue edition (1 June 1976).

we descend into our own living hell we are descending into God and into holy mystery, for there is no place where God is not.

Where shall I go from your Spirit?
Or where shall I flee from your presence?
If I ascend to heaven, you are there!
If I make my bed in Sheol, you are there!
If I take the wings of the morning
and dwell in the uttermost parts of the sea,
even there your hand shall lead me,
and your right hand shall hold me.
If I say, 'Surely the darkness shall cover me,
and the light about me be night',
even the darkness is not dark to you;
the night is bright as the day,
for darkness is as light with you.

Psalm 139:7–12

My Nanny Emerson, a woman of immense godliness, fortitude and devotion, often quoted her favourite verse to her grandchildren: 'remember son, underneath and all around are the everlasting arms.' She would paraphrase further to make the point: 'you can't get below his arms, son!' We can't escape God. Not all our answers will come, but silence does not mean absence. Even the darkness is not dark to him, to him the darkness is as light. It is crucial that as we experience the silence of heaven we affirm these strong arms of God holding us even when we have no strength to hold him.

SILENCE FORMS US

These thoughts and reflections on silence and the embrace of mystery prompt the question 'does our quest for certainty actually stunt our growth?'

In many streams of the church today we seem to lack a coherent, robust and honest engagement with suffering, confining it to the margins of our preaching, liturgy and discipleship. Consequently, we are missing out on some beautiful things God *can do* with our suffering. In times of crisis the temptation is to simply 'pull ourselves together', and press on stoically into the future. We fill our lives with things that will help us feel that we are moving forward, and in doing so reinforce our certainty of life. We resort to flimsy understandings of God, 'let go and let God' or 'don't worry, God's got a perfect plan', or even worse 'God just needed another angel in heaven'. This childish faith, incubated in unchallenged and protective environments, prevents any true steps to maturity, and is unhelpful to those who are suffering. Certainty is a perversion of true faith. Personal security in life is an illusion. As Helen Keller said, 'life is either a daring adventure or nothing'.[18] We will be broken in this life and our natural response is to want to make ourselves believe we are ok before we really are. We want a shortcut through the pain. But there is a time in life for all of us where it is ok *not* to be ok. And what if the pain is teaching us something that we dare not rid ourselves of before it works its way through us to a place of healing? Rohr provocatively asserts: 'resurrection will always take care of itself, if death is to be trusted ... It is the cross, the journey into the necessary night, that we must be convinced of, and the resurrection is offered as a gift.'[19]

In James's epistle to the church he encourages the early believers during times of persecution to remain steadfast, even 'Count it all joy' (James 1:2) for something purer and deeper is being perfected and refined. There is a redemptive silver lining. *The Message* translation captures the essence of what I am trying to articulate in this chapter.

> So don't try to get out of anything prematurely. Let it do its
> work so you become mature and well-developed,
> not deficient in any way.
>
> James 1:4 MSG

---

[18] Helen Keller, *Let Us Have Faith*, Doubleday & Doran & Co. Inc (January 1940).
[19] Richard Rohr, *Adam's Return: Five Promises of Male Initiation*.

Suffering, and in particular the silence of God we may experience in times of deep suffering, can therefore be the path to mature holiness. What if prayerful silence, while initially infuriating, is actually a gift? A gift of gracious space where our suffering can be redeemed into something transformative, not stunted or patronized?

Before I follow this through, allow me an important disclaimer. I am not comfortable with the view, implied by some, that we should cosy up to suffering, make friends with it because God, like a hard-headed Victorian school teacher or strict army general, gets a buzz out of teaching us something the hard way. A 'no pain, no gain' theology isn't what I am talking about here. We must remember suffering is an intrusion into God's good world and will have no part in the new heaven and earth. Sickness is something we pray against as true followers of Jesus. Suffering is not a virtue. We should resist all pious attempts at over-spiritualizing our suffering as it has led many to a detestable sort of veiled conceitedness. All our thoughts need to be framed in the wider narrative of God's great story of redemption:

- God's desire to rescue his beautiful creation from its rebellious intentions and deathly consequences;
- his desire to reinstate his loving and wise reign over humanity and the inauguration of his reign through the life and teachings of Jesus;
- the conquering of sin and the defeat of the tyrant through the death and resurrection of Jesus reversing the effects of the fall and revealing the first fruits of new creation;
- the re-empowering through the indwelling of his Spirit in his image-bearers commissioned to pray and proclaim the coming of the kingdom of God on earth;
- the final and supreme act of God that awaits us when God will bring both heaven and earth together in perfect harmony eliminating forever sin, suffering and death, where 'God will be all in all'.

It is precisely because of this – God's victory, God's supreme redemption of humanity through the whole sweep of history – that all our suffering in this present world cannot compare to the glory that will one day be revealed in us. We may have the signs of the wounds we endured on earth in our resurrected bodies, but like the holes in the hands of the resurrected Jesus these wounds will speak only of victory. Everything is redeemable in Christ, everything can be made whole and beyond our imaginations, all of what we give to Christ will only be ennobled and glorified in the age to come. Suffering, therefore, is not our friend. Our hearts join the chorus of groans from all of creation, longing for the supreme and final act of God's glorious victory when all strivings and suffering will cease. It is important our reflections are held within this worldview.

Yet, as the Bible confirms, God does sometimes permit times of testing and tribulation. Suffering, while not from God, can become a means that God uses in mysterious ways to reveal his glory. Once, when the disciples were questioning Jesus about the suffering of a blind man:

> And his disciples asked him, 'Rabbi, who sinned, this man or his parents, that he was born blind?' Jesus answered, 'It was not that this man sinned, or his parents, but that the works of God might be displayed in him.'
>
> John 9:2–3

And the apostle Peter reminds us: 'Yet if anyone suffers as a Christian, let him not be ashamed, but let him glorify God in that name (1 Peter 4:16). We are encouraged to be sensitive and discerning, ensuring we don't short-circuit the process. The Bible instructs us how to *endure* suffering in this world, while at the same time affirming the great hope that one day all suffering will end. 'Is anyone among you suffering? Let him pray. Is anyone cheerful? Let him sing praise' (James 5:13). This is my underlying hope for this book: as we experience suffering in this world and as we endure the silent and seemingly mute days of heaven we would, perhaps more than in any other season of life, PRAY! That we would call on God, honestly, relentlessly, and daringly. First of all, in simplicity and with brevity, we cry out to him to help us make it through the night. Then, as we sense his gentle touch and compassion, we would ask for his will to be done, for his kingdom to come, for his glory to be revealed. As Brother Lawrence encouraged:

> Be courageous. Offer your pains to God. Pray for strength to endure. Above all, develop a habit for conversing often with God. Adore him in your infirmities. At the very height of your suffering, ask him humbly and affectionately (as a child to a good parent) to help you accept his will.[20]

Something much greater is going on, a weight of glory beyond what we can imagine. Endure the silence, for as St John of the Cross concluded: 'to come to the pleasure you have not you must go by a way in which you enjoy not.'[21]

Jesus 'learned' obedience

To emphasize the point, here is an often-neglected verse in the Bible found in the letter to the Hebrews:

> Although he was a son, he learned obedience through what he suffered. And being made perfect, he became the source of eternal salvation to all who obey him.
>
> Hebrews 5:8–9

The writer to the Hebrews tells us that Jesus himself, although wholly perfect in nature and sinless in word, deed and thought, was learning obedience, becoming full-grown in maturity through the testing-ground of suffering. As John Stott, commenting on the redeemable nature of suffering, declared: 'if the sinless Christ became mature (through suffering), so much the more do we need it in our sinfulness.'[22] John Stott, St James, St John of the Cross, Brother Lawrence, the writer to the Hebrews and countless other testimonies both past and current,

---

[20] Brother Lawrence, *The Practice of the Presence of God*, Hodder & Stoughton (11 June 2009).

[21] St John of the Cross, *The Ascent of Mount Carmel*, Aeterna Press (11 May 2015).

[22] John Stott, *The Cross of Christ*, InterVarsity Press (1986).

present us with the hope that waiting in prayer, enduring and engaging our hearts with the silence of suffering leads us to perfection and maturity worth more than fine gold. And if Jesus didn't take a shortcut through this process, neither should we.

The message of the kingdom of heaven is that victory and triumph come *through* suffering and enduring the silence of God. Our theology is complete only if it includes both a theology of celebration *and* suffering; prayers are complete only when God hears our pain *as well as* our victory. If theology really is 'faith seeking understanding'[23] it is those of us who have lived through suffering that bring deeper understanding, nuance and richness to genuine faith. Rushing to the Easter 'Resurrection' Sunday can prevent us from receiving the divine energy found in Friday and Holy Saturday. There is luminosity breaking through the darkness of these hours.

This is my faithful and honest testimony. Think about it. Various names have been offered throughout history to name Easter Saturday – for example, 'Black Saturday' and 'Easter Eve' – but *Holy* Saturday is how most of us refer to this day in the Christian calendar. I love this. I love that the in-between, the place of deafening silence is called *Holy.* I love that God lived through a Saturday – he waited it out – resurrection came only after the suffering was taken seriously. Barbara Brown Taylor puts it beautifully: 'New life starts in the dark. Whether it is the seed in the ground, a baby in the womb, or Jesus in the tomb, it starts in the dark.'[24]

The wounded places in our hearts, the silent caverns of our souls, the dark tunnels of our minds, are the hiding places of God. It therefore follows that if we let him in, in time these places become the birthplace of creativity and all things new. Silence endured points towards an even greater revelation yet to come. No one ever imagined in the darkness and silence of Saturday how spectacular Sunday would be.

Through all of this, paradoxically God is purifying our faith by threatening to destroy it. We are led to a profound and holy distrust of

---

[23] This was the famous motto of St Anselm, *fides quaerens intellectum.*
[24] Barbara Brown Taylor, *Learning to Walk in the Dark.*

all superficial drives and human strivings. We know more deeply than ever before our capacity for infinite self-deception. Slowly we are being taken off vain securities and false allegiances. Our trust in all exterior and interior results is being shattered on we can learn faith in God alone. Through our bareness of soul God is producing detachment, humility, patience, perseverance.[25]

YAHWEH

The incomparable, omnipresent, omnipotent, God of the universe, who is outside of time, has a name – I AM. In Moses' burning bush experience, in Exodus chapter 3, God for the first time reveals his *personal* name. God's personal name is simply four vowels – YHWH. Theologians call this the *tetragrammaton*, which literally means 'four letters', and it is from these that theologians derive the name Yahweh. Some theologians propose that when we phonetically voice these four letters slowly and rhythmically we pronounce sounds that most resemble the sounds of our breathing. The implication of this is staggering – we are never closer to saying the most revered and personal name of God than when we are simply breathing. Inhale and Exhale = Yahweh. Our very breath is breathing his name. As Psalm 104 confirms:

> When you hide your face, they are dismayed; when you take away their breath, they die and return to their dust. When you send forth your Spirit, they are created, and you renew the face of the ground.
>
> Psalm 104:29–30

Our breath is his breath. Could it follow that one of the indicators of God's 'veiled' presence in our experience of silence is enveloped in the next breath we breathe?

---

[25] Richard Foster, *Prayer: Finding the Heart's True Home*.

Wait in prayer and breathe. He is waiting for you, and you too will come to testify that silence does not mean absence.

The very name of God, Yahweh, and its derivation and meaning reveals a deeply significant dimension of the character of God. 'I am who I am' or 'I will be who I will be' are the closest translations theologians propose. When God reveals himself to Moses he is essentially saying, 'You can't box me in, I am beyond your limits, your control, your efforts to reduce me to the confines of your own intellectual capacity'. God's encounter with Moses allows us to conclude that the God who is beyond our comprehension and definitions is the God who is closer than our breathing. 'God is both further from us, and nearer to us, than any other being', C.S. Lewis concludes.[26] These characteristics of God must be held in equal tension. God's immanence and immutability are two sides of the same coin. He is ultimately majestic but irrevocably approachable: 'Nothing is too great for his power, nothing is too small for his love.'[27]

In our pain and suffering God is not answering our questions, for we come to learn that they are beyond the objective explanations our rationalized minds crave. God reminds us, *I AM* in the midst of the flames – and that, we will learn, is more than enough. God doesn't give us answers. In the silence he gives us himself, bigger than our pain, beyond our explanations, closer than our breath. Silence leads us to a more excellent way of knowing, which we will now explore in more depth – the paradox of life *and* death bound together in the heart of God.

---

[26] C.S. Lewis, *The Problem of Pain*, William Collins (19 November 2015).

[27] David Watson, *Is there Anyone There*, Hodder & Stoughton Religious, 5th impression edition (1 October 1983).

CHAPTER SEVEN

PARADOX

I have come that they may have life, and have it to the full.

John 10:10 NIV

AFRICAN HEROINES

I love Africa! Over the years I have travelled to different parts of the continent, banking myriad memories of the most life-giving of times. The playfulness of the children; the joy and laughter of the rural pastors; the hands of the hard-working labourers. But the most endearing, vivid and poignant memories of Africa are the beautiful and weathered faces of the old women. In every village there are a handful of ageing, frail, half-crippled ladies, unobtrusively observing the life of the community. The quiet weight of their presence always humbles me.

When I see these women sitting in the background, stirring porridge over a crackling fire, I feel a magnetic draw. As I sit down near them, they will try to engage me in conversation, the one or two English words they know mixed in with their own tribal language. This playful conversation usually ends in laughter as we struggle to understand one another. Usually they want to thank me for coming to their village to help. The irony of this is that I always end up receiving far more than I give in these African communities.

As I look into their eyes I feel as though I am peering into the pages of a story, deeper and richer than anything I have ever read. I am mesmerized by the lines in their faces, the coarseness of their hands and the white light of their eyes, telling of all they have endured. Living in a traditional patriarchal culture, these women would have known severe hardship along with the burden of rural homemaking. Severe poverty, losing babies in childbirth, surviving genocide and burying their husbands – behind the lines, etched into their faces, are stories of heartache and grief. Yet somehow I am not overwhelmed with sadness when I speak to them. Despite the roughness of their hands and the deep lines in the tight black skin of their faces, I see remarkably defiant women smiling, with a glint in their tired eyes. I am conscious of the sadness they have endured, I sense heartache, yet there is resilience. I come alive as I draw strength and energy from these women. They radiate the most authentic type of life I have witnessed, as they carry both the wounded and wonderful around in their weary bodies.

These faces, I came to realize, personify enigmatic beauty. The place where truth is unearthed in startling radiance. They are a personification of a luminous darkness. As I returned to Africa after Lindsay's passing, days spent sitting by a pot of porridge, looking into these women's lined faces, allowed me to connect with something so soulful and authentic it unknotted my tangled innermost thoughts. The questions, doubts and emotional wrangling subsided in a beautiful way. In their company I found a deeper connection of truth by simply being *present* with them. The paradoxical nature of their lives, revealed in the lines of their beautiful faces, granted me fresh permission to process my grief with a resourcefulness I struggled to find elsewhere. Looking into their eyes brought healing and the first inklings of hope.

These African heroines taught me that the process of leaning into pain, of truly grieving before God, leads us into a deeper wholeness. It is in faces like theirs that we discover the paradoxical nature of the heart of the Christian faith.

As these days of luminous darkness continued to dismantle my Sunday school Christian worldview, the borders of my faith were being expanded, stretched and reshaped. I was emerging with a new perspective, something beyond the black-and-white, compartmentalized thinking

I had been used to. I find myself reflecting now on how the Christian tradition I was brought up in often insulates itself from engaging with the real contradictions we face in the day to day, humdrum of life. Life itself is a paradox much up of equal doses of hopeful anticipation and fear, 'filled simultaneously with heartbreaking sweetness and beauty, desperate poverty, floods and babies, acne and Mozart, all swirled together'.[1]

Going through these dark days, however, wasn't merely intellectual reflection – rather I was forced into this tension – searching and scrambling for something *more*; something more authentic, more whole. My grief journey was now drawing me into an integrity more profound, a truer understanding of humanity, and this involved holding together the questions of life on this earth, by the grace of God. I had been intrigued by the contradictions and paradoxes in Christian doctrine in a cerebral way in the past, but it was only when death flattened me that I came to realize that technical knowledge means nothing when your heart is in pieces.

For those who are edging out of the darkest parts of their own grief tunnel, who are beginning to believe Resurrection Sunday may just be possible, understanding the paradoxical nature of life and faith is crucial if you want to walk right through the tunnel, into wholeness. When we discover how this dynamic is central in the life and death of Jesus we can bring ourselves back from the dead.

ORTHODOXY

While Lindsay and I were dating, I read G.K. Chesterton's classic book, *Orthodoxy*. Chesterton's fascination with the nature of paradox won him the nickname 'the Prince of Paradox'. Where the critics of the day had argued that the scriptures contained contradiction and incongruent juxtapositions, Chesterton countered by articulating

---

[1] Anne Lamott, '12 Truths I Learned From Life and Writing', https://www.ted.com/talks/anne_lamott_12_truths_i_learned_from_life_and_writing.

the beauty and genius of paradox at the heart of Christian faith. It is precisely the paradoxical shape of Christian doctrines, Chesterton would contend, that allows it to answer deep and moral questions about our existence. He would have been a fan of the apostle Paul's conclusion of the paradox at the heart of the gospel: 'For the foolishness of God is wiser than human wisdom, and the weakness of God is stronger than human strength' (1 Corinthians 1:25 NIV).

Consider the paradox of original sin. Christianity holds that mankind is the chief of all living creatures *and* the chief of sinners. Chesterton called this the doctrine of normal abnormality: by nature, humans are able to experience the glory of highest value and the awe of meekest humility.[2] We could spend a whole chapter looking at other examples: God is both three and one; Jesus is both human and divine; when we are weak then we are strong. As Elton Trueblood advised, 'If a man wished to avoid the disturbing effect of paradoxes, the best advice is for him to leave the Christian faith alone.'[3] Christianity, as Chesterton and others have advocated, is a religion of higher truths.

PARADOX IN SCRIPTURE

After Lindsay's death, I found that Chesterton's arguments for paradox began to underpin my new and evolving understanding of suffering. Waiting in the silence and trying to embrace the mystery of God, I found a seemingly opposing and contradictory blend of emotions coursing through the Bible. The Psalms in particular provided the language I needed to express my own personal paradox.

Psalm 6 begins full of impassioned lament, desperation and resignation:

> Be gracious to me, O LORD, for I am languishing;
> heal me, O LORD, for my bones are troubled.

---

[2] Chris Hauser, *Faith and Paradox: G.K. Chesterton's Philosophy of Christian Paradox*, The Dartmouth Apologia, Volume 6, Issue 1 (Fall 2011).
[3] Elton Trueblood, source unknown.

> My soul also is greatly troubled.
> But you, O LORD – how long?
>
> Turn, O LORD, deliver my life;
> save me for the sake of your steadfast love.
> For in death there is no remembrance of you;
> in Sheol who will give you praise?
>
> I am weary with my moaning;
> every night I flood my bed with tears;
> I drench my couch with my weeping.
> My eye wastes away because of grief;
> it grows weak because of all my foes.
>
> Psalm 6:2–7

And it then shifts to hope, defiance and confidence:

> for the LORD has heard the sound of my weeping.
> The LORD has heard my plea;
> the LORD accepts my prayer.
>
> Psalm 6:8B–9

These words of the Psalmist echoed my own heart cries:

> God, I still love you but I am angry with you.
> God, I can't feel you but I know you are here.
> God, I can't understand you but God, you are my only hope.

The apparent contradiction of these emotions was disconcerting, but gradually I was learning that this contradiction was closer to real life, and the life of God's people throughout history, than I had previously understood. Tom Wright describes the paradoxical nature of many of the Psalms:

> This is the place of intense pain and intense joy, the sort that perhaps only music and poetry can express or embody. The Psalms are gifts that help us not only to think wisely about the overlaps and paradoxes of time, but to live within them, to reach out in the

day of trouble and remind ourselves – and not only ourselves but also the mysterious One whom the Psalms call 'you' – of the story in which we live.[4]

It is worth pausing for a moment to remind ourselves that the Psalms we often read so lightly are holy songs and prayers which have been around for thousands of years. They are the raw material that formed Christ's own prayer life and they are of immeasurable worth to us, for they capture the now-and-not-yet experience of the people of God. They help us live more fully as image-bearers of God in the paradoxes of our time. For Chesterton was right: paradox is at the heart of Christianity. An incomparable juxtaposition – Cross *and* Resurrection. We cannot emphasize triumph and victory at the expense of suffering on our sojourn here on earth. The Psalms (and other Wisdom books) give us a song to sing at this point where Cross and Resurrection meet.

I came to realize that all the seeming contradictions within me didn't necessarily have to cancel each other out. Rather, in holding both with an equivalent tension, I discovered a kind of holy nuance, an enriched understanding of the truth, enabling me to see life in a more truly spiritual and holistic way. Richard Rohr put it like this: 'The truth in paradoxical language lies neither in the affirmation nor in the denial of either side, but precisely in the resolution of the tug of war between the two.'[5]

It was this 'paradox epiphany' that began easing me towards a new place of orientation in my journey of grief. My fear had been: *in accepting Lindsay wasn't coming back, how was I to hold all I had experienced, in my head and my heart, for the rest of my life?* It felt uncomfortable and unresolved to settle for a neat definition and compartmentalization of such a tragedy. Now though, through my 'Holy Saturday' days of engaging contemplative prayer, I was finding a new way to hold what appeared to be counter-arguments together with equal tension.

---

[4] Tom Wright, *Finding God in the Psalms: Sing, Pray, Live*, HarperCollins (2014).
[5] Richard Rohr, *Richard Rohr's Daily Meditation: Paul as Non-dual Teacher* (Sunday 5 April 2015).

God didn't cause this to happen, yet God was still in
  control;
God was suffering with me yet God was my healer,
Jesus was asleep in the boat yet Jesus was calming the
  storm.
I could feel vulnerable, fragile and alone, yet closer to
  God than ever.
God doesn't 'heal' everyone but God is THE ultimate
  healer.
God is light and yet he dwells in deep darkness.
The kingdom is both now and yet not yet.

I was enjoying a fresh sense of permission to hold these things in my heart with a holy curiosity and attitude of inquiry. There was a renewing of my mind, a fresh perspective. I could begin to contemplate walking forward into freedom. Rainer Maria Rilke encapsulates something of the spirit of my paradoxical discovery in these famous words:

> Be patient toward all that is unsolved in your heart and try to love the questions themselves, like locked rooms and like books that are now written in a very foreign tongue. Do not now seek the answers, which cannot be given you because you would not be able to live them. And the point is, to live everything. Live the questions now. Perhaps you will then gradually, without noticing it, live along some distant day into the answer.[6]

THE PARADOXICAL JESUS

As we might expect, the paradoxical nature of Christianity intensifies and comes into sharper focus in the teaching and life of Jesus. Jesus' teachings and parables draw from the prophetic and wisdom tradition and they drip with beautiful irony, mainly because his intention was to show us what the world really looked like on *his* terms.

---

[6] Rainer Maria Rilke, *Letters to a Young Poet*, Random House Inc (27 December 2001).

'the first will be last and the last shall be first.'

'he who wants to save his life will lose it but he who loses
his life for my sake will find life.'

Jesus came to reorder the world around an axis of love, humility and servanthood, as opposed to power, status and greed. To do so he had to confront our fixed and ingrained thought patterns of justice and entitlement by inviting us to see beyond our dualistic thinking. Things aren't usually black and white. We aren't asked to enter into a system of beliefs, we are invited to surrender our hearts to a PERSON.

Jesus did not provide us with an explanation for evil and suffering. Jesus refused to fit in with the social constructs, formulas and technical explanations of his day. It has been observed that Jesus answered only three of the 183 questions that were asked of him! Instead of answering questions about pain and suffering Jesus meets us where it hurts the most and absorbed that pain into himself. As N.T. Wright describes: 'He doesn't allow the problem of evil to be the subject of a seminar. He allows evil to do its worst to him. He exhausts it, drains its power, and emerges with new life.'[7]

Jesus will not use an abstract theory to free us from our fixed minds and self-centeredness. Rather, he will fully enter into the pain of life and redeem it at Calvary, showing us that the 'foolish' paradoxical nature of his death on the cross is indeed the power of God unto salvation. Christ crucified: the power and wisdom of God (1 Corinthians 1:24). Instead of providing us with neat and rational explanations, Jesus provokes us towards wisdom, to another way of thinking, a way beyond control to a way of *participation* in the 'rollercoaster of life and death'.[8] Jesus invites us to lay our lives down, like he did, if we really want to find life. This is the paradox at the heart of Jesus' life and the centerpiece of the gospel. This is life in all its fullness.

[7] N.T. Wright, *Simply Good News: Why the Gospel Is News and What Makes It Good*, HarperOne (6 January 2015).
[8] Richard Rohr, *Adam's Return: Five Promises of Male Initiation*.

LIFE IN ALL ITS FULLNESS

The scripture, more than any other, which for me held all of these contradictions together was John 10:10 (NIV), 'I have come that they may have life, and have it to the full.' As I contemplated this verse prayerfully through the dark night of my soul, I couldn't deny that, in a strange way, the experience of grief and of leaning into pain was becoming mysteriously life-giving. In the midst of brokenness, there was depth and meaning which was illuminating and, dare I say at this point, transformational.

For many years I had held the youthful and naïve position that life in all its fullness was the feel-good factor, the upsurge of emotion, the buzz one 'got' after an adrenaline-fuelled worship gathering, where we reminded one another how 'on fire' we were and high-fived one another for Jesus. But as the years rolled on and I became a little bit more reflective in my faith journey, I remember wrestling with this verse with one of my friends, John, a few years before Lindsay's illness. Life was becoming much more nuanced, our naïvety and innocence unpicked, as we grappled with injustices surrounding us. Surely life in all its fullness must be more than simply being 'pumped up' for Jesus, the Christian version of being 'high'? These reflections were forced upon us through difficult circumstances.

In the summer of 2005, we mobilized young people in our town to unite and demonstrate their faith in practical ways in the poorest parts of our communities. It was an incredibly satisfying and life-giving week, watching our discoveries about the message of the kingdom lived out in front of our eyes. We finished the week encouraging all the young people that this was life, in all its fullness!

The day after that week of joy, we learned that a young man called Mark, who had been coming to our church, had taken his own life.

Mark had been troubled most of his life. A few weeks earlier he had come to church and given his life to Jesus. At first this brought him strength, but life continued to be a torment for him, and then he ended it. We were devastated. I was asked to do the funeral. It had been a tremendous week with the mission projects but, I reflected, I was experiencing no less a sense of God's presence as I dealt with Mark's death. It was different, of course, but God *wasn't* different. He was as present as he had ever been. Searching for words I found myself drawn to Gethsemane and Jesus' final hours, where he experienced unfathomable torment. The synoptic gospels describe Jesus' agony of soul as 'overwhelmed with sorrow to the point of death' (Matthew 26:38 NIV). I began to imagine Jesus in those moments facing a sorrow and torment that almost killed him. It dawned on me, powerfully: Jesus has been there. He would understand what Mark's torment felt like. While devastated by Mark's choice to end his life, I found a wave of compassion for him well up inside me. I realized I was experiencing something deep – I was 'feeling' God's heart for Mark. I was experiencing his presence even more acutely than I had the previous week, when I had danced with a hundred young people enthused by the Holy Spirit. I became aware of something I have never forgotten. God was the first to cry at Mark's death. He is there in the dancing and he is there in the dying.

The experience helped me to see that life in all its fullness is much more than a spiritual buzz. Pursuing happiness alone, often what contemporary popular Christianity settles for, is a poor substitute. Jesus is inviting us into the reality of being ALIVE, fully ALIVE, through *all* the seasons of life. He is inviting us to know his very life, to carry his own heart, to embody his actual nature, in every circumstance of life and to overflow with this kind of life in the world. Apart from Jesus I'm not sure anyone experienced and articulated this better than the apostle Paul. He understood his life's mission as a living paradox, 'always carrying in the body the death of Jesus, so that the life of Jesus may also be manifested in our bodies' (2 Corinthians 4:10). This is life in all its fullness – *his* life in us – which means on the one hand experiencing the sheer delight of seeing God's kingdom come in ways that transform, heal and redeem, and on the other hand experiencing the pain of the Father watching humanity suffer the consequences of our deviation from his loving intention for us.

Heaven certainly isn't boring. Imagine the depth of emotion tasted in the heart of the Godhead every living moment of time – the incomparable joy of his image-bearers taking on his nature, reflecting his glory, displaying hope and healing in the world. Yet imagine the anguish and grief he experiences watching his image-bearers broken by sin and suffering. The pain he contends with through the rejection of those he loved from the beginning.

Following Jesus is no mere 7-out-of-10 lifestyle. Following Jesus is a life of the highest highs and deepest depths – the extremes of God's heart pulsing in a fully surrendered human heart.

To share the heart of God, both the joy and the pain, I came to learn, is a deep and holy privilege. I could not rush my Holy Saturday experience. As a teenager I had once fervently and genuinely asked God to 'give me his heart' to 'break my heart for what breaks his', 'to share his heart with me so I would really *know* him'. Now, God was teaching me a whole new depth to what Paul described as the 'excellency' of knowing him, 'that I may know him and the power of his resurrection, and may share his sufferings, becoming like him in his death' (Philippians 3:10).

To know Jesus is to know life, his life. This means the awesome privilege of knowing his resurrection *and* his suffering. It's the space we find ourselves most days even though we often try to get through life simply on the surface of things – but we can become aware that this paradoxical space is *sacred space*. This is why when I look into the eyes of these African women I know I am enjoying a 'spiritual' connection. Their faces and their lives are sacred spaces. A living embodiment of the Psalms and the life of Jesus – celebration and sorrow held together in the powerful love of God. As I think about the back story of their weathered faces I see the 'not yet'. I am reminded that while Jesus inaugurated the rule of his kingdom on the earth through his life and death and resurrection, all of creation still groans in expectation for the full consummation of his victory.

Suffering, sickness and death are realities. Yet in the smiles of these women I also see the 'now', I become aware of heaven interlocking and breaking into our broken world bringing healing, dispelling darkness, offering redemption and purveying hope. The world is sad and beautiful and in these women I see clearer than ever that beautiful paradox. They may be old, bent over, wrinkled and poor, yet they carry something beyond this world. Their lives personify the intersection of time, their faces carrying the song of God's 'now-and-not-yet' people. All truth is a paradox.

CHAPTER EIGHT

REORIENTATION

You cannot work on the structure of your life if the ground
of your being is unsure.

Christian Wiman[1]

'The world for which you have been so carefully prepared is
being taken away from you,' he said, 'by the grace of God.'

Walter Brueggemann[2]

The silent response from God enveloped the space in the middle of my
grief tunnel, stretching out over several months. These were days of
profound self-discovery, illumination and the beginnings of rebirth.
As I embraced the paradoxes and slowly learned to trust this process,
my soul began muscling itself into a new space while my mind searched
for a reconstructed paradigm for life and faith. The fragile process of
reorientation lay ahead.

---

[1] Christian Wiman, *My Bright Abyss: Meditation of a Modern Believer.*
[2] Walter Brueggemann via Barbara Brown Taylor, *Leaving Church: A Memoir of Faith,*
HarperOne, 1st edition (1 May 2012).

GAP YEAR

At the age of eighteen, I went away to 'find myself'. I left home and embarked on that quest – more commonly known as taking a gap year – after a profound encounter with God during my final year of school. A revelation of his love flash-flooding my heart had left me with an insatiable hunger simply to know him more, and a thirst for adventure in faith. I went to live and work in a shelter for street kids on the outskirts of Johannesburg, in Lenasia, a place which had been a tightly bordered Indian township under the apartheid regime. I didn't know what to expect – I simply felt God was inviting me to leave home to go and find him. Naïve, perhaps, but to me a response of simple obedience.

I boarded a plane wrapped up in sadness at leaving my close-knit family, and landed in South Africa not even entirely sure who was picking me up. I could not have known that what lay ahead of me, ten thousand miles from home, were ten of the best and most difficult months of my life. But the first thing that hit me, as the only white person living in a street-kid shelter in a township, was the culture shock. While I loved working with the children, I was desperately missing friends and family, crippled by loneliness, aching for home.

Then came a bigger shock. I began to realize that I didn't *know God* nearly as well as I had thought. I had been brought up in a Christian home, had memorized almost half of the Bible, and was under the illusion that I knew God quite well. In South Africa I came to see that … I didn't. I knew a lot *about* God. But I didn't *know him*. I knew him only by association. It was a tough reality to face, in a foreign land, far from my church and closest friends, washing out of a bucket and eating chicken feet for dinner!

My over-confident presumption, drawn from a childhood steeped in a slightly pious church environment, that my relationship with God was so profound it would spur me on to great adventures in my gap year, was exposed. I came to the uncomfortable realisation that my knowledge of God was merely *associated* with other parts of my life – bound up in relationships and routines, in friends, school and church. When these had been removed, and all that was left was God and me, I began to see how little I know him. It was a significant rite of passage and I stumbled through it, but persevered. With none of the vocabulary that I now have to articulate the experience with, and with no similar previous experience to draw on, I leaned into the loneliness and disorientation, knowing I had to endure these difficult months in order for something new to be formed in me.

I found resonance at that time of my life with the words of Jeremiah chapter 1. The passage affirmed, despite my loneliness, the calling and destiny I was beginning to sense:

> Before I formed you in the womb I knew you,
> and before you were born I consecrated you;
> I appointed you a prophet to the nations.

> Jeremiah 1:5

In that scary, lonely place, removed from everything familiar, I was also drawn to a verse further on in the chapter:

> See, I have set you this day
> over nations and over kingdoms,
> to pluck up and to break down,
> to destroy and to overthrow,
> to build and to plant.

> Jeremiah 1:10

These lines intrigued me, 'to pluck up and to break down, to destroy and to overthrow, to build and to plant'. The word order of Jeremiah's assignment caught my attention. 'Plucking up', 'breaking down', 'destroying and overthrowing' all came *before* 'building and planting'. Deconstruction was required before true construction could take place. Shaky foundations needed to be replaced before anything lasting could be built. Or, as Barbara Brown Taylor put it, 'sometimes the salvation of the psyche begins with its own demise'.[3]

---

[3] Barbara Brown Taylor, *Learning to Walk in the Dark*.

As I became aware of the excavation process going on in my heart, I embraced it, if a little reluctantly, scrambling desperately for a fixed reference point to set my identity around. It was a sore and unwelcome reality but, as I stuck it out, it became a season of monumental growth and formation for me as a person and a follower of Jesus. I began to build a faith that was deeply personal, true and real. A revelation of the Father heart of God started to transform me and I began to cultivate my own personal relationship with him, beyond what had been simply passed down to me from my parents. From the initial disorientation and bewilderment of stepping off a plane into a country I had never been to before, a culture completely foreign to my own, and a realization I didn't really know God, I started to form something genuine, deeply true and authentic. It became a foundational bedrock for life and leadership in the following years.

DECONSTRUCTION

When Lindsay died, eight years later, it felt as though, once again, everything was demolished. The foundations had just about survived – I had a degree of certainty that the Father I had come to know in a street-kid shelter on the outskirts of Johannesburg still loved me. But everything else was shattered, broken in pieces. The 'walls' of the worldview I had built for my 27-year-old life crumbled around me and I was hopelessly trying to clear away the rubble. The architectural supports, the pillars and props I had used to construct these walls – the promises from the Bible – seemed cracked, shot through with fault lines. Favourite texts that I had founded my faith on, staked my life upon, were in question; every promise from scripture was now uncertain; every verse I had memorized was hanging in the balance. The frame of reference for my faith had been dismantled; the scriptures that had brought comfort and strength during Lindsay's sickness now seemed hollow as I stared into the reality of widowerhood. I still had a foundation of faith, even a genuine love for God, but I just didn't know how to rebuild anything on that foundation, because every opportunity for believing again was overshadowed by a giant question mark.

I was now undergoing another rite of passage, only this time it registered somewhere off the charts! With no explanation for my 'underserved' suffering forthcoming, I came to understand that the preconditions I had put on my relationship with God were being ruthlessly examined and found wanting. As in the story of Job, it wasn't only God who was in the dock. The silence from heaven had gently exposed my heart. I found to my surprise – and initial denial – that the image and expectations of God I had formed were a projection of my own wants and desires. I talked to my old theology professor, Stephen – one of the wisest men I had ever met – about the questions that continued to haunt me:

I thought God would bless me if I honoured him?

Why would it be any better for anyone, even God, for Lindsay to be dead?

What do I do with the Biblical principle of sowing and reaping? Because my experience is that this just doesn't hold true. I sowed good 'kingdom' seeds and look what I reaped – sheer devastation.

Stephen listened and affirmed my questions, deliberately and empathetically. At one point he said something I will never forget. He looked at me with gentle candour and said: 'Alain, we often come to learn in life that sometimes our journey towards God is a stripping away of illusions about God.'

I can still feel the tender force of these words. It was precisely the road I was walking – stumbling – along. I was journeying towards God but my assumptions, what I had decided about the ways that he should act towards me, were being exposed and challenged. I was becoming aware of an uncomfortable truth – I had subconsciously held God hostage with my prayers. I had predetermined how God should honour me in my life and assumed a posture of *entitlement* – the reason it felt like God hadn't come through was because, quite simply, he hadn't met *my* agenda. It felt like a part of my ego, a part that

I didn't even realize was there, had been exposed. In the words of the assumed heretic and French mathematician Descartes, I was realizing 'that once in life I would have to raze everything to the ground and begin again from the original foundations'.[4]

I realized I had to surrender my preconceived ideas of *how I expected God to act towards me*. I needed to learn to trust and believe in him outside of the agenda I wanted him to fulfill. I needed help to think this through, to find a new reference point, something around which I could discover fresh meaning for the rest of my life. I referred again to Elie Wiesel's classic, *Night*. Wiesel's journey of 'losing-God-to-find-God', his gravely moving narrative describing the experience of living through the Holocaust, was a perfect companion for the dark path I was walking. Wiesel had been forced to question everything he knew about God, as the most ghastly of horrors happened right in front of his eyes. Among the most devout of Jewish children, he loved God dearly. Yet in those terrible days, the faith his childhood was steeped in was so completely deconstructed that he could only conclude: 'Never shall I forget those moments, which murdered my God and my soul and turned my dreams to dust. Never shall I forget these things, even if I am condemned to live as long as God himself. Never.'

Wiesel's stark reflections resonated deeply with my deconstructed soul. Like him I had loved God all my life, now I was trying, like Wiesel did, to reconstruct a new way of knowing him, a way of restoring trust in him. I prayed out my confused and inarticulate prayers to God:

> Father, what do you actually guarantee in this life? I think you guarantee that you will never leave us or forsake us, that you will always love us, that nothing can separate us from your love, that you are for us and that you are our healer. But how do we hold to your promises in scripture without predicting the future? How much do you really give revelations that guarantee something about our future anyway? I think you can do this ... but, as Stephen said, maybe this is more the exception

---

[4] René Descartes, *Meditations on First Philosophy*, OUP (8 May 2008).

than the norm. And if this is only the exception, is it to prevent us from having faith in conditions and promises, rather than faith in you alone?

As I picked myself up and sought to go about the 'reconstruction' of my faith, I began to realize that the foundations I had established as a 19-year-old in the back streets of Johannesburg had more substance and strength to them than I had originally given them credit for. Building on this foundation I was helped by Walter Brueggemann's commentary, *Spirituality of the Psalms*. The Psalms had become a lifeline for me by then. Brueggemann suggests a dynamic interrelatedness in the Psalms, a scheme for an overarching approach: *orientation – disorientation – new orientation*. His implication is that the anatomy of the Psalter corresponds to the seasons of the human soul.[5]

- *Psalms of orientation* help describe those seasons that evoke gratitude for God's consistency, faithfulness, unchangeableness and steadfastness. They speak of things like creation, wisdom, the Torah and the favour of God. Some examples are Psalms 1, 8, 19, 33, 119.[6]

- *Psalms of disorientation* are a response to those seasons of life involving heartache, anguish, alienation, suffering, and death. They are known as the Psalms of Lament and Complaint. Some personal complaint Psalms are Psalms 3, 6, 55, 88.[7] Some communal Psalms of Lament are 60, 74, 126, 137.[8]

- *Psalms of new orientation* express a type of surprised joy which has broken through the despair, where we become aware of a 'fresh intrusion', a gift from God that bring us out into a new place. Some examples are Psalms 18, 30, 40, 138.[9]

---

[5] Walter Brueggemann, *Spirituality of the Psalms*, Augsburg Fortress, abridged edition (25 February 2002).
[6] Other Psalms of Orientation include 14, 15, 104, 131, 133 and 145.
[7] Other Psalms of Personal Complaint (Disorientation) are 5, 7, 13, 17, 22, 25, 26, 27, 28, 35, 39, 41, 42, 51, 54, 56, 57, 59, 61, 63, 64, 69, 71, 86, 102, 109, 130, 140, 141 and 143.
[8] Other Psalms of Communal Lament (Disorientation) are 79, 80, 83, 90 and 124.
[9] Other Psalms of New Orientation are 34, 65, 66, 124 and 129.

Brueggemann is careful to refrain from rigidly categorizing our lives into one particular season, but rather recognizes the constant movement from one circumstance to another in life, and all the emotions and reactions that are produced in our souls as a response. For the Psalmists, all human emotion, in fact all of life itself, was brought under the rule of God.

DISORIENTATION: NAVIGATING THE LIMINAL SPACE

The place of disorientation, this place of 'in between' that many of the Psalms so powerfully give voice to, is known by academics as the place of *liminality*. The word has the same root as the word *limbo*. A 'liminal space' is a concept born out of studies in anthropology and refers to a transitional period of life. Victor Turner, the originator of the concept, was studying the dynamics of coming of age rituals and principles of initiation. He was interested in the place between 'child' and 'adult' where an individual is neither one nor the other. Those who can remember the precarious path of adolescence will remember the daunting nature of such an indeterminate and uncertain place. Alan Hirsch and Michael Frost describe liminality in their book *The Faith of Leap*:

> It is composed of any or a combination of danger, marginality, disorientation, or ordeal and tends to create a space that is neither here nor there, a transitional stage between what was and what is to come. As a result it is experienced as a place of discomfort and agitation that requires us to endure and push into what is to come.[10]

These phrases – 'what was and what is to come'; 'neither here nor there'; 'discomforting and agitating' – describe exactly the see-sawing of emotions I was experiencing. This 'discomforting and agitating'

---

[10] Michael Frost and Alan Hirsch, *The Faith of Leap: Embracing a Theology of Risk, Adventure & Courage*, Baker Books (15 April 2011).

in-between stage is intensified by the fact that one feels completely different to everyone else in this moment. This is the loneliness of the liminal space. Transition is hard. No one else gets it. You are trying to find your way somewhere new when everyone else, it seems, is doing normal things. As I alluded to earlier in this book, the best analogy I can find of the felt-emotion during this period of liminality is one of intense homesickness. It is the feeling of overwhelming emptiness following you around, aggravated by separation, in the case of losing a loved one, from the people who you know could remedy it. I wasn't sure where 'home' was any more. Home for me had become the place where Lindsay was, and now she was gone I felt not only homesick but homeless.

I was groping around in the vagueness of the in-between, seeking out a new place of orientation, trying to find something to hold on to. I was clutching at thin air as the fixed things I had perceived about God were now stripped away and dismissed as illusory. Jonathan Martin describes it candidly: 'sometimes it feels like the walls are closing in, because the house you've built for your faith really is too small.'[11] The liminal space isn't much fun. It doesn't make friends with security, the type of security that is badly needed to soothe the daunting fear of the future. And it reveals our fragile independence. I began to learn that an act of courage is needed, and an embrace of the paradox I explained in the previous chapter, for there are great temptations hovering around, offering to fill the void with something else. Sometimes the temptation is to find something external to numb the pain and distract us from our 'real' thoughts: a superficial relationship; a damaging distraction; or a running away. And then sometimes the temptation is from within, a practised protective mechanism to repress and bury questions, where God (and everyone else) is refused access. Despite some flirtations with these temptations I couldn't shake the conviction that wholeness would come only through a sustained posture of leaning into my emotions, embracing the paradoxical nature of them and straining my eyes to see Jesus standing in the middle of them.

---

[11] Jonathan Martin, via Twitter, https://twitter.com/theboyonthebike.

NEW ORIENTATION

Enduring these days of liminality by praying Psalms of disorientation and sitting before the Lord, I began to experience fleeting moments of revelation. I didn't always like the revelation, but it ensured a flow in the process of reconstruction and reorientation. I found a new language, through what Brueggemann describes as the 'fresh intrusion' of hope, in the Psalms of reorientation.

> He sent from on high, he took me;
> he drew me out of many waters.
> He rescued me from my strong enemy
> and from those who hated me,
> for they were too mighty for me.
> They confronted me in the day of my calamity,
> but the LORD was my support.
> He brought me out into a broad place;
> he rescued me, because he delighted in me.
>
> Psalm 18:16–19

It was the beginning of a new orientation, a gentle leading into a broad and spacious new place. Without understanding what this looked like I was simply opening my heart again to the unrelenting delight of God in me.

TRUE COLOURS SHINING THROUGH

In retrospect, despite the instability of this liminal space, it was here that I learned most about myself. Suffering has a proven record of forcing reflection on us in a way that softens us and changes us. 'You know that under pressure, your faith-life is forced into the open and shows its true colors' (James 1:3 MSG).

Faith that is forced into the open shows its true colours. Suffering exposes what we really think about things – God, life, ourselves. As my friend Stephen had implied, suffering and grief were revealing more about me than they were about God. The questions that I was asking God were, in quite disarming ways, rebounding back on myself. As C.S. Lewis described: 'God has not been trying an experiment on my faith or love in order to find out their quality. He knew it already. It was I who didn't!'[12]

It may be helpful here to recall the story of Job. The first three quarters of his book appear to have God in the dock, as Job seeks to grieve and process his tragic loss, protesting and questioning God. In the final pages, however, we find Job himself on trial. It turns out that God asks good questions too. As I alluded to earlier in the chapter, I had to take my turn in the dock.

Without realizing it, we can quickly find ourselves serving God for ourselves rather than out of love for him. The true colours of my faith were being revealed and I became ever more aware of my own self-serving agenda. It is through such times of testing we often see the selfishness underpinning our expectations of God. Barbara Brown Taylor puts it eruditely: 'in the dark, you see how shabby a faith based on benefits really is.'[13] Your faith-life if forced into the open shows its true colours.

Religion based on meritocracy is a sham religion! No matter how much we have heard about grace, our faith can often be subconsciously constructed upon the principle of transaction. Underneath our piety it is a self-centered projection of how God should act, based on what we have done for him, or how 'good' we have been for him! Richard Rohr describes this mindset as a 'closed system' that divides the world into 'deserving' or 'non-deserving'. Jonah's reactions against God's merciful response to Nineveh's repentance is a revealing example of humanity's distorted views of justice and entitlement. The reality is, life is much

---

[12] C.S. Lewis, *A Grief Observed.*
[13] Barbara Brown Taylor, via a sermon she delivered at the 2014 Festival of Homiletics in Minneapolis, Minnesota http://time.com/110734/sermon-series-entering-the-dark-cloud-of-god/.

more mysterious and nuanced than our narrow binary understanding of blessing and punishment. God is not 'the cosmic enforcer of karma, making sure we get what we deserve. God is the one who interrupts this cycle with grace.'[14] The conditions of God's promises can be fully realized only in a complete surrender to his wondrously mysterious grace-filled ways. We need a revelation of the 'absolute gratuity of grace' and 'undeserved character of mercy' if we are to walk out of this soul-confining meritocratic way of thinking.

The complete dismantling of my previously 'well-orientated' place forced me to ask questions I never would have had to answer if I had not suffered. The result was a new place of orientation where I began to hold even more lightly to things I had previously thought I had control over. God only knows where the wind is going to blow. I concluded there is little God guarantees in life outside his covenantal, unfailing love, the steadfast inherent goodness of his character, and the promise of his presence. Yet in my luminous darkness I came to realize proper revelation of these is more than enough! I comprehended more deeply than ever: *everything* I had in life came from him. There wasn't anything less true about the promises of God in scripture I had so rigorously questioned just because *my* experience hadn't turned out the way *I* wanted it to. God was indeed still the God who honoured those who honoured him and the principle of sowing and reaping was still active and alive in the universe. *How* God honoured me and *what* I reaped were simply not my prerogative.

REVELATION THROUGH SUFFERING

In recent years I have found the teaching of the Jesuits, particularly the spirituality of St Ignatius, to be wonderfully helpful on the revealing of self through suffering. For St Ignatius, suffering was not something we should desire in a kind of ascetic aspiration towards higher spirituality

---

[14] Jonathan Martin, *How to Survive a Shipwreck, Help Is On the Way and Love Is Already Here*, Zondervan (2016).

but, when suffering comes, we should recognize how God uses it to detach us from the excessive self-interest we subconsciously allow to control our thinking. By leaning into our pain we become aware of this shallow imposter resident in our feelings. Subsequently and graciously we can be liberated from this and encounter the face of God. New birth is waiting on the other side. Deeper levels of righteousness, joy and peace are ours to enjoy. If this is the end, then suffering is only the means. Disorientation will give way to a new and glorious orientation: 'He brought me out into a broad place; he rescued me, because he delighted in me' (Psalm 18:19).

His gentleness exposes our mercenary thinking through suffering and yet, in his tender and audacious ways, as we surrender all over again to him, he leads us into greatness beyond what we could imagine for our lives. With such a glorious end awaiting us we dare not allow ourselves to repress the questions and the pain. We dare not escape the disorientated place before we learn what God can teach us through it. Remember James's words to us, 'don't try and get out of anything prematurely'. God is making us into the kind of people that look like Jesus.

SEASONS: THE ACT OF LETTING GO!

For the most part, life itself is an act of letting go. Somewhere in life each one of us is going to 'die' before we die. Trying to 'stay in control' will only stunt growth and sabotage the new life pregnant within. The world is not static and neither are we. God's character is reassuringly immoveable, but his Spirit is always moving. Christianity itself is a movement and so we as his image bearers should be caught up in *his* moving. Seasons are set into the very fabric of creation itself and hardwired into our souls. As Jonathan Martin describes: 'Creation is in a constant cycle of unpredictability, death, beauty, new life, all yielding from the "chaosmos" in James Joyce's phrase.'[15] This is one of

---

[15] Jonathan Martin, via Twitter, https://twitter.com/theboyonthebike.

the reasons why Jesus' main methods of teaching was to tell stories and parables. He was seeking to shock people out of their wrong mindsets, their old and meritocratic patterns of thinking. He was inviting them out of their mentality of entitlement into a God-immersed reality. Martin contends: 'Christianity isn't a belief system – belief systems all crack under pressure. It's a way of seeing the world that, once seen, can't be unseen.'[16]

The ancient wisdom of the scriptures prepares us for such. The earthy wisdom of the writer of Ecclesiastes reminds us that 'for everything there is a season, and a time for every matter under heaven' (Ecclesiastes 3:1).

Understandably, there was a time for me to be consumed with my own story of acute grief. But eventually I came to realize that all of humanity passes through these seasons of life – new birth, planting, healing, building, weeping, laughing, mourning, dancing, hating, loving, tearing, sowing, seeking, losing, dying – and as we do, a recurring pattern emerges.

We are constantly letting go and becoming new.

The question is 'will we let go?' We can choose not to. We can choose to hold on to a past season of life and consequently let it define us. There had been a time in my life when to honour Lindsay was to love her with every fibre of my being, 'as Christ loved the church'. I look back knowing I gave her every part of me I possibly could have. Then there was a time when to honour Lindsay was to grieve her absence wholeheartedly in body, soul and spirit. Then there was a time when to truly honour her was to let her go. I would never forget, I would carry her in my thoughts for the rest of my life, occasionally when appropriate I would take out photographs and celebrate her life and the beauty of what we had. I would look forward with great joy to seeing her in heaven. But I needed the wisdom of God to help me realize that the physical, tangible, real-life connection we enjoyed on earth could not sustain me in this life, even though I tried for months. I needed the courage of God to help me realize that this chapter of my life was over and only monumental

---

[16] Jonathan Martin, via Twitter, https://twitter.com/theboyonthebike.

amounts of his grace could help me move into a new season. He gently graced me for such.

I understand why people find it so difficult to make this choice, but I also know that in holding on to the past we are choosing to cap the pain, live in denial and stunt our growth. Fear, anguish and shame – the main causes of our resistance to change – will only create self-perpetuating cycles of accommodation for our pain, eventually resulting in cynicism, apathy and bitterness. *Remember: pain that is not transformed will be transmitted.* The courage of letting go may leave us initially lonely and disorientated but in the long run only in embracing such a transition will we experience a whole new place of orientation. We are dying to our old 'selves', letting go of our old mindsets, our protected identities and our selfish illusions to become more of our true 'selves'.

Whatever secret disappointment you are carrying, whatever loss you have never fully grieved, whatever injustice you have never voiced, God is waiting to hear it and transform it if you let him. We don't have to live with a tortured mind and a closed heart forever. It isn't easy but only in letting go can you cling more tightly to him.

THE STABLE WITNESS

Don't allow anything to stop you from what you are becoming. Voice the pain whatever way you need to but don't let it stop you from becoming all God is making beautiful in his time. The primary way we ensure we move through these changing seasons towards freedom is through prayer! Abiding in God – the 'Stable Witness'[17] – in times of shaking. Recognizing the tensions within your soul, voicing the painful and confused contradictions to the Father. Letting him hold you in the midst of it. This is prayer at its most primal and most powerful. The Psalms continue to prove a faithful map on our

[17] I came across this term in the works of Richard Rohr.

journey. They give us 'a window into the bright lights and dark corners of the human soul'.[18] They remind us that in 'limbo' we are uncomfortably revealed yet loved no less. Trusting God but doubting God, loving God but questioning God, hoping for a better future yet consumed with the pain of our current reality. We are letting go of constructs and mindsets that have given us an illusionary sense of security, but in exchange we get him. Only his presence can untangle the thoughts of our minds and the hidden griefs of our hearts reorienting our lives to a place where we can contemplate a hopeful future.

NEW NAME

As I began moving into a place of new orientation, I remembered a conversation I had with my counsellor, Andrea. While I had been relaying the intensity of this struggle to trust in God and the ongoing divine wrestling match that had ensued, she reminded me of what Jacob wrestled himself *into*. The result of this gigantic God-tussle was more than a quick hip replacement. Jacob wrestled himself into a new identity confirmed by a new name. Jacob wrestled God until God could make something new out of him.

Jacob became 'Israel' – a 'Prince with God' and subsequently the name given to God's chosen people, Jacob's descendants. I always find it enthralling that the signature name of the people of God, through whom God would work his redemptive purposes for the world, came because of a wrestling match with a flawed and twisted man. Think about it, a good old honest scrap with God was the birthplace of the identity of the covenant people chosen by Yahweh to be a 'light to the nations'.

God knew the kind of man Jacob could become. God had an original design for Jacob and he was relentlessly committed to seeing this 'deceiver' become all he dreamed he could become. It is sheer joy

---

[18] Tom Wright, *Finding God in the Psalms: Sing, Pray, Live.*

to realize how committed God is to us and how seriously he takes the prayers we pray and the songs we earnestly sing.

We have great company in this journey. The pages of the Bible tell story after story of individuals experiencing a metamorphosis through grief, pain, failure and disappointment towards beauty, destiny, true purpose and ultimately Christ-likeness. In all these stories, their most significant times of transformation came through seasons of disorientation, disillusionment and disappointment.

When we have nothing left to give God but our shell-of-a-being, it is then we are most qualified to serve him. Abram and Sarai learning to trust God's promise despite infertility and years of barrenness become *Abraham* and *Sarah*, the great patriarchs of our faith; Joseph surrenders his feelings of betrayal and unforgiveness to God and becomes the most influential leader in the world; Simon overcomes the guilt of failure and damaged pride to become *Peter*, the 'Rock', on whom the Church is built; Saul surrendering a life of high-powered Jewish religion and intellectual pride becomes *Paul* the apostle and the mobilising force behind the spread of Christianity to the Gentile world. Each found out that in letting go they would truly become. They all had been dismantled and reconstructed into lives of greatness.

We must not read these accounts of Biblical characters in a patronizing way, as simple, flat Sunday school stories. We need to stop sanitizing the Bible. We need to allow *these* real broken lives to inspire *our* real broken lives. In seasons of bareness, smashed ideals, betrayals, and loneliness we too can step into the big God story and experience the same flow of redemption. God will never invalidate your pain, but when you face up to him with all you have, he will begin the process of making something beautiful.

Nine years after I had previously come to understand it, as a 19-year-old in South Africa, I was learning, in an even more dramatic way, that in life there is often a 'plucking up and breaking down' before there is a 'building and planting'. Those who hope in God through the cycle of orientation–disorientation–new orientation make it through the dark night of the soul with the purest of gold to show for it.

CHAPTER NINE

HOPE

Another world is not only possible, she is on her way, on a
quiet day, I can hear her breathing.[1]

Arundhati Roy

May the God of hope fill you with all joy and peace as you
trust in him, so that you may overflow with hope by the power
of the Holy Spirit.

Romans 15:13 NIV

SURPRISED BY HOPE

Hope surprised me. It didn't come as I expected. It wasn't a heavenly
vision descending from the skies with beautiful plans for the rest of my
life. But one day I heard the birds singing, and like a butterfly landing
gently on my hand, there was a simple awareness that I was alive
again. A little like the inconspicuous, sporadic and almost clandestine
nature of Jesus' resurrection appearances, the first shoots of life burst
through with gentle surprise. Grace, I reflected, was surreptitiously
tiptoeing its way through my being, opening the windows of my soul

---

[1] Arundhati Roy, *War Talk*, South End Press, 1st edition (1 April 2003).

to more light. I became conscious of a quiet joy rising in my heart in response to extremely ordinary things. The swelling waves of grief became less frequent, and the periods of calm became longer. I had come through the wild rapids and now was able to gather myself a little as the breakers subsided around me.

At first, hopeful thoughts carried undertones of guilt. Would hoping again lead to a diminishing of what Lindsay and I had enjoyed? Yet there was a growing assurance that Lindsay was now completed, whole. As I pondered where Lindsay was and what she was doing, I noticed that the pining in my heart to be united with her on earth was less intense. A distinct peace, reflecting on her wholeness in paradise, grew in the deep parts of my soul. As I became more sure of this, it slowly began to dawn on me that the *worst* thing I could do was to pretend that, by wallowing in my loneliness, I could keep our love alive. She was completed by a love we had glimpsed together, particularly in the last months of her life on earth. The purity of our love matured and returned to me as an empowering presence, permitting me to hope again, permitting me even to love again.

To people who haven't lived through this kind of loss, it may seem more 'loyal' not to move on, better to fight to keep one's love alive. But I realized there would be something disingenuous and frankly unrealistic about such an endeavour. My experience was teaching me there was a valid counter argument to be made: choosing not to love again would almost dishonour the fullness of the love Lindsay and I had enjoyed. Christian Wiman explains:

> many people fight hard to keep their wound fresh for in the wound, at least, is the loss and in the loss the life you shared. Or so it seems. In truth the life you shared, because it was shared, was marked by joy, by light ... Excessive grief, the kind that paralyzes a person, the kind that eventually becomes an entire personality – in the end this does not honor the love that is its origin.[2]

The depth of love Lindsay and I had encountered through the months of suffering was a selfless love. A love, liberating and freeing, not

---

[2] Christian Wiman, *My Bright Abyss: Meditation of a Modern Believer.*

possessive and manipulating. I stood at Lindsay's grave and reflected that Jesus had allowed Lindsay and me to share something of himself. The nature of our love in those difficult days of Lindsay's sickness was a reflection of God's immeasurable love towards me. I knew her love, now fully subsumed into his love, was a love that was *FOR* me and *FOR* my future rather than a pseudo-love serving only to imprison and immobilize me for the rest of my life.

I had the distinct impression that Lindsay was cheering me on, giving me the playful wink of approval that she used to do when she was alive. We had embraced everything God had for us in the short time we had together. We had given each other everything we had to give. C.S. Lewis reflected on the short but intensely happy season of oneness he experienced with his beloved Joy:

> It could also mean 'This had reached its proper perfection. This had become what it had in it to be. Therefore of course it would not need to be prolonged.' As if God had said, 'Good; you have mastered that exercise. I am very pleased with it.'[3]

MOVING FORWARD

By this stage I was probably less conflicted in my own motives than I was worried about how other people might perceive 'moving on'. Phil had taught me that there are lots of people who want to cry with you in pain, but not everyone wants to rejoice with you when it's time to rejoice again. Everyone will have an opinion, but in the end only you know, deep down, what the place of new orientation looks like. And you know it only by taking it one day at a time, working it out, prayerfully, with your Father who fashioned all of the days of your life before you had even lived one day (Psalm 139:16). Lean on him. You are breaking new ground, tentatively discovering a new normal. People can give helpful advice, but unless they have been there they

---

[3] C.S. Lewis, *A Grief Observed*.

don't really know what it is like. The Spirit of Truth, your Advocate, is the only truly reliable Guide.

In our church we have observed that people who have never fully voiced their disappointment, rage and pain – people who have never truly leaned into their pain – often find it easy to enter into the sorrow of others, but distinctly difficult to fully embrace the healing of those who choose to journey *through* their grief into a new, hopeful place. Pain can become our primary place of identity and many who have suffered, unfortunately, choose not to leave that place. Christian Wiman warns us of such a position:

> Be careful. Be certain that your expressions of regret about your inability to rest in God do not have a tinge of self-satisfaction, even self-exaltation to them, that your complaints about your anxieties are not merely a manifestation of your dependence on them. There is nothing more difficult to outgrow than anxieties that have become useful to us, whether as explanations for a life that never quite finds its true force or direction, or as fuel for ambition, or as a kind of reflexive secular religion that, paradoxically, unites us with others in a shared sense of complete isolation: you feel at home in the world only by never feeling at home in the world.[4]

I imagine the place Wiman is warning of as like sitting in a prison cell. After a period consumed with your own pain, grief and doubt you realize that the door is now open, someone has opened it. Of course it is going to take time to reintegrate into the real world and the prospect is daunting, overwhelming. But the door is open. You don't have to stay there. To your surprise, some of the people who have been with you in the cell, providing companionship and support, don't want to walk out with you. The thought of freedom seems to scare them. In their eyes you see a sad resignation, a belief that their own disappointment is too difficult to overcome. Hope is too costly. Worse than this, they have become visibly uncomfortable with the fact you want to leave. It seems your freedom is their loss.

But I couldn't stay there. C.S. Lewis described how, later in his journey, the door of heaven that had been bolted shut in the early

---

[4] Christian Wiman, *My Bright Abyss: Meditation of a Modern Believer.*

days of his grief 'no longer seems locked'.[5] I had been true to the feelings of pain, anger and injustice in my darkest of days, now I had to be true to the glimmers of hope I was experiencing. I didn't try to manufacture hope. I never intentionally thought about hope, or even forced myself to be hopeful. Rather, being true to the reality of the pain, facing up to the disappointment I was experiencing, dealing with it honestly before God, seemed to carry carry me into this place. In giving voice to lament and protest, I found a true language for hope and promise.

Trusting the process of death and transformation before the face of the Father will always result in resurrection. He can be completely trusted for victory, if we can trust him in our pain. Like dawn stealing away the darkness of night, slowly and naturally, hope begins to rise.

THE NATURE OF HOPE

New life breathed on me and, gradually, different possibilities for my future opened up: my football, my friendships, my ministry and maybe someday even another soulmate. While the stubborn, brutish part of me occasionally wanted to push hope away, I realized in doing this I was denying something primordial within me. The ancient wisdom of the Proverbs confirmed this to me:

> Hope deferred makes the heart sick,
> but a desire fulfilled is a tree of life.
>
> Proverbs 13:12

If living without hope makes us sick, the implication of Solomon's wisdom is that we are created with a natural capacity, a need to hope. We are image-bearers of a *hope-full* God:

---

[5] C.S. Lewis, *A Grief Observed.*

> hope is there within and among us for we are ordained to be a
> people of hope. It is there by virtue of our being in the image
> of a promissory God.[6]

The original glory of humanity innately possessed the virtue of hope. To be fully alive is to be hope-filled. It follows that when we are hope-*less* we are *less than our true selves*, we are deficient, we are 'sick'. We can't avoid disappointment in life, and we are certainly not immune to it, but the greater truth is that we are created for hope. Seasons of disappointment will come, we should expect them, and we may go through times when disappointment is a deeply real experience – but it should not become our fixed position. Hope should be our default mindset, our go-to theme, the soundtrack of our lives. Hope can become a constant for the child of God. The apostle's punchy refrain to the young church in Rome enforces the point: 'Rejoice in hope, be patient in tribulation, be constant in prayer' (Romans 12:12).

During the early days of the grief our church endured through the passing of Jill and Lindsay, Psalm 84 became a biblical place of reference for us, in particular the 'Valley of Baka' which means literally the Valley of Weeping.

> Blessed are those whose strength is in you,
> whose hearts are set on pilgrimage.
> As they pass through the Valley of Baka,
> they make it a place of springs;
> the autumn rains also cover it with pools.
> They go from strength to strength.
>
> Psalm 84:5–7 NIV

For months we had centered our thoughts on the emptiness of this valley, unable to move from this deep ravine, daunted by the steep cliff faces either side, yet acknowledging his silent presence in the midst of it. As time passed and we returned to this Psalm, we discovered that the Valley of Baka was not our final destination. It is most certainly

---

[6] Walter Brueggemann, *The Prophetic Imagination*, 2nd revised edition, Augsburg Fortress (June 2001).

a real and treacherous valley, and we had a sacred language, soul-companions and the presence of Jesus to help us pass through. But notice, the Valley of Baka is a place we *pass through*. As people whose hearts are set on pilgrimage we, like our father Abraham, are walking, sojourning, travelling, not always knowing where we were going, but with growing faith go from 'strength to strength'. Hope is both our compass and our destination. Not only is hope the resident theme of our story, it also shapes and forms our very souls. As Dostoevsky surmised, 'to live without hope is to cease to live'.[7]

RISKY HOPE

For many who have endured the brutal realities of grief, pain, ongoing suffering and constant disappointment, this talk about hope might sound a bit like pie in the sky. I want to say something about this that I trust will help. Hope, I have found, is often lauded in ways that doesn't acknowledge the concrete nature of pain many people carry. It can be reduced to glib optimism from the positive-thinking school of pop-psychology; it is an ideal that Christians talk and preach about, but it is often completely removed from the harsh actuality and searing nature of real loss. It even undermines the truth. If this is your experience, hope may seem to you a kind of distant fairytale ending, a forced utopia, a product of superficial or fanciful thinking. I have lived through these doubts myself, doubts concerning the authenticity of hope, while developing a mild cynicism towards how it is sometimes referenced in the relative comfort of western Christianity.

The gradual reawakening of hope in my heart was completely unnerving. Hope in the in-between, in the liminal 'now and not-yet' nature of limbo, is a beautiful but precarious virtue. When the soul has been damaged so completely, putting your hope in anything or anyone again is a risky business. This is why many stay in the prison cell.

[7] Fyodor Dostoevsky, source unknown.

> What if this new hope crumbles down around me causing
>   even more pain?
> What if this hope is only another illusion of a new life?
> What if I gave myself to something else or someone
>   else and it simply resurrects the loneliness I am trying
>   to overcome?

Hope, in this fragile place, can be the best of things and the worst of things. As much as I didn't want to move on without Lindsay, I also didn't want my grief to define me forever. For the broken-hearted, hope is the most courageous of acts, as it involves choosing the incomprehensible – choosing to leave the past and believe in God's future without knowing where it could lead. It was an act of will and a step of faith to choose to lean into hope, believing the goodness of God could still be a reality and not just wishful thinking.

As well as courage, hope takes perseverance. While I could contemplate and process hope, it often felt like one step forward and two steps back. Hope would rise that my football career would get back on track, but I would find my body still not ready to compete; hope would stir that I could integrate into my friendship circle again and enjoy life but, in a crowded fun-filled environment, loneliness would regularly creep up and I would languish again in despair; hope would even grow that another woman would come into my life to rescue me from my loneliness, and then I would realize that some of the girls I was beginning to feel attracted to just weren't Lindsay. In each of these scenarios the disappointment felt so much more severe than in more normal circumstances. My desperation for something to hang my dreams upon meant that often my expectations were over-emphasized. As I chose to strain for a new normal, I found hope had a way of both lifting my gaze and disappointing me in equal measure. It was also exhausting emotionally. True hope, I was learning, possesses backbone, resilience and a certain defiance.

Nevertheless, that revelation from Proverbs 13 – 'Hope deferred makes the heart sick; But when the desire comes, it is a tree of life' – implied that *not* to hope would ultimately mean closing my heart unnaturally. Shutting hope down would be the *less human* thing to do.

It would mean my *choosing not* to hope and that would mean staying detached from love, beauty and ultimately life itself through the rest of my life. This wasn't really a great alternative and our faithful fellow pilgrim, King David, inspired me on. 'I would have lost heart, unless I had believed that I would see the goodness of the LORD in the land of the living' (Psalm 27:13 NKJV).

Hope, I was learning, was not simply to be found in a better set of circumstances – rather, hope was fundamentally and intrinsically centred in a Person.

GENUINE HOPE

The authentic language of the praying saints of the scriptures had helped me find expression for my pain. Now I was discovering they wouldn't let me stay there for the rest of my life. The Psalms, while ruthlessly honest with their current tribulations, don't leave us destitute forever. They don't allow us to wallow in our pain. Rather they seem unable to repress a deep anticipation for God to break through as he alone epitomized the hope of their very existence. These prayers had spoken tenderly and empathetically to the turmoil of my soul, but now they were declaring hope and rebirth.

> For you have delivered my soul from death,
>   my eyes from tears,
>   my feet from stumbling;
>   I will walk before the LORD
>   in the land of the living.
>
> Psalm 116: 8–9
>
> When the LORD restored the fortunes of Zion,
>   we were like those who dream.
> Then our mouth was filled with laughter,
>   and our tongue with shouts of joy;
>   then they said among the nations,

'The Lᴏʀᴅ has done great things for them.'
The Lᴏʀᴅ has done great things for us;
we are glad.
Restore our fortunes, O Lᴏʀᴅ,
like streams in the Negeb!
Those who sow in tears
shall reap with shouts of joy!
He who goes out weeping,
bearing the seed for sowing,
shall come home with shouts of joy,
bringing his sheaves with him.

Psalm 126

Jürgen Moltmann describes the hope these wonderful Hebrew writers espouse in scripture: 'Genuine hope is not blind optimism. It is hope with open eyes, which sees the suffering and yet believes in the future.'[8]

I love the integrity of the 'genuine hope' the Bible offers us. A 'hope with open eyes' is a hope that never invalidates the suffering we are experiencing, but rather encourages us to 'pray it', acquiescing with us through the pain and eventually helping us see beyond it. The hope of which the Bible speaks captures both the holy tension of the wounded and the wonderful essence of life on this earth. Only 'hope with open eyes' can find it. Eugene Peterson lucidly describes the blend of hope, lament and humility the Biblical authors achieve majestically: 'The timing is important. If the terminus is proposed too soon, people know that their suffering has not been taken seriously and conclude that it is therefore without significance.' Conversely, if it goes on too long, he argues, it becomes 'a crippled adjustment to life that frustrates wholeness'.[9]

There is no formula, no one-fits-all timeframe for this journey into hope. Our Father, who has known us from our mother's womb,

---

[8] Jürgen Moltmann, *Experiences of God*, SCM Press (1980), 14.
[9] Eugene H. Peterson, *Five Smooth Stones for Pastoral Work*, Eerdmans, reprint edition (31 December 1996).

loves us uniquely and tenderly. He knows what we need, and when we need it, and his timing is perfect for us. We must lean into him to know this holy tension and allow his perfect timing to lead us into wholeness.

CHOOSING TO HOPE

It was the freedom that came through my honest prayers in the time of suffering that empowered me to fix my gaze upward and then forward.

Any faith I had for the future was formed on praying verses 25 and 26 of Psalm 73 more than any other: 'Whom have I in heaven but you? And there is nothing on earth that I desire besides you. My flesh and my heart may fail, but God is the strength of my heart and my portion forever.'

My heart and flesh had failed, and only God could defibrillate my heart. Genuine hope continued to rise through simply choosing to believe some of God's promises *even when I didn't feel like believing them*. It is like going to the gym when you want to lie on the couch, drink a beer and scoff a packet of Monster Munch. It requires the deliberate activation of feeble faith muscles – muscles you don't even realize are there until they are exposed. There is no time for forced self-analysis or pious moralizing. I couldn't allow religious despair to become a 'defense against boredom and the daily grind of existence'.[10] I needed to choose to believe in something, or, more accurately, someone. I had to *do* something. I had to live and believe my way into a new place.

There comes a point when you are going to have to simply choose to believe God is who he says he is, even when you don't *feel* like believing him. God is drawn to movement. Sometimes that movement is risk-taking and daring faith for a change-the-world dream. But sometimes that movement is more earthy, humdrum and elementary

---

[10] Christian Wiman, *My Bright Abyss: Meditation of a Modern Believer.*

– the straightforward choice to keep living, to not give up, to keep walking even when it hurts like hell.

HOPE AND FAITH

In Biblical thinking, hope and faith appear as inseparable virtues. More well-known words from Romans open this up to us vividly:

> … we have also obtained access by faith into this grace in which we stand, and we rejoice in hope of the glory of God. Not only that, but we rejoice in our sufferings, knowing that suffering produces endurance, and endurance produces character, and character produces hope.
>
> Romans 5:2–4

Hope is born out of persevering faith, when everything around us is hanging in the balance. At some point the circumstances of life will force upon you an intense period of face-to-face, heart-on-the-sleeve rhetorical questioning of God.

'God, either you are who you say you are or you aren't.'
'Either you work everything together for good or you don't.'
'Either you bring beauty for ashes or you don't!'
'Either you make all things beautiful in your time or this is just a nice phrase for a sympathy card!'
'Either you still have good plans for me or I am out!'

I couldn't sit on the fence any longer so I *prayed* these make-or-break prayers to God, with passion and intensity. It was a time for raw, undiluted, faith-stimulating prayers that required an act of will; trusting myself *into* the character of God and believing my way *into* a hope-filled future. I can't emphasize this enough. With all the bloody-mindedness and determination you can muster, there are periods of life when you simply have to stake everything on the promises of God for your future. Chuck all the poker chips in. Double or quits. All or nothing. I can testify, God is worth the risk.

Inspiration for this kind of faith again comes in the everyday characters of the God-story, none more so than Abraham, the nomad, called by the Lord to carry his dream for the world. To this random, childless old wanderer, God gave a promise that the whole earth would be blessed through his offspring. Such effrontery! Whilst sin had been multiplying around the earth since the fall, God had called Abram to reverse this by multiplying blessing. There was only one problem. He was a hundred years old and Sarai, his wife, was ninety. He couldn't multiply anything. But, despite the reality of human impossibility and absurdity of this candidate for such a destiny, Abram *contended* for the promise of God. Yes, he made mistakes along the way, but Abram staked his life on this promise. He directed the honest anguish of his soul to Yahweh when it seemed as though there was no way the promise could be fulfilled, 'O Lord GOD, what will you give me, for I continue childless ... you have given me no offspring' (Genesis 15: 2–3). This is another example of the honest prayer of complaint, rising from a forsaken soul to the Father. Despite the reality of his hopeless circumstances staring him in the face, Abram continues to hope in the presence of Yahweh – his 'shield, and ... exceeding great reward' (Genesis 15:1 KJV). It is a faith, staring into the reality of barrenness and brokenness, still choosing to believe for the impossible. The apostle Paul, writing to the Romans, is keen to extrapolate for us this extraordinary faith of Abraham that we are all called to:

> That is why it depends on faith, in order that the promise may rest on grace and be guaranteed to all his offspring – not only to the adherent of the law but also to the one who shares the faith of Abraham, who is the father of us all, as it is written, 'I have made you the father of many nations' – in the presence of the God in whom he believed, who gives life to the dead and calls into existence the things that do not exist. In hope he believed against hope, that he should become the father of many nations, as he had been told, 'So shall your offspring be.'

He did not weaken in faith when he considered his own body, which was as good as dead (since he was about a hundred years old), or when he considered the barrenness of Sarah's womb. No unbelief made him waver concerning the promise of God, but he grew strong in his faith as he gave glory to God, fully convinced that God was able to do what he had promised. That is why his faith was 'counted to him as righteousness.' But the words 'it was counted to him' were not written for his sake alone, but for ours also. It will be counted to us who believe in him who raised from the dead Jesus our Lord, who was delivered up for our trespasses and raised for our justification.

Romans 4:16–25

Abram 'hoped against hope'! Beautiful poetry, gutsy faith! Even when there was no hope, Abraham continued to hope. This was heart-thumping, honest, backs-to-the-wall, grit your teeth, genuine faith. This was a journey of faith with no map, only a compass. He alone wants to be our true north. No wonder Paul called Abram, 'Father Abraham', not simply because of his 'many sons' but for the way he epitomized the very heart of Judeo–Christian faith, believing in the God 'who gives life to the dead and calls into existence the things that do not exist' (Romans 4:17). One cannot but admire the earthy and hearty pragmatism at the heart of the God story. The Bible teaches us that hope that is merely seen is no hope at all. Rather we contend for that which is not yet.

Fast forward to the first pages of the New Testament and we are introduced to a similar character of resolute hope, in the life of a prophetess called Anna, a woman waiting to see the promise of the Messiah. Anna was married for seven years before she lost her husband and since that time lived as a widow for eighty-four years.[11] At this point Anna was 'advanced in years', likely over a hundred. Yet

---

[11] There is some ambiguity to how Luke seems to dwell on Anna's age and there is conjecture amongst scholars. Her widowhood has either lasted 84 years or she is 84 years old when she crosses the Biblical stage. There are also some scholars who argue: Anna married at age 14, evidently a common age, was widowed at age 21, and then meets the young family 84 years later aged 105.

she served God 'with fasting and prayer night and day' not departing from the temple.

I have a fond place in my heart for Anna. She lost her soulmate when she was young. Yet after eighty-four years of widowhood, Anna never lost hope, putting herself in a place where she hungered to see what, to that date, God had only given her a glimpse of. Despite the brokenness, the loss, the regret and the loneliness that must have imposed themselves upon Anna's soul throughout those years, she never let cynicism, disappointment or apathy settle in her heart, stifle her joy or diminish her expectation. When Jesus was brought to the temple as a baby to fulfill the customs and be presented before God, Anna 'began to give thanks to God and to speak of him to all who were waiting for the redemption of Jerusalem' (Luke 2:38). I imagine the venerable Anna, throwing her walking stick down, and unashamedly losing herself in worship, as the hope she had clung to for eighty-four years was realized in the baby Jesus. Every bone in her tired and faithful body surely leapt for joy.

The Bible leaves little space for wallowing in self-pity. In Jesus, God identifies with our pain, in that lonely garden of Gethsemane when he sweated great drops of blood for us. In the fullness of his humanity he made a choice, and in doing so demonstrated a faith that requires movement – setting his *face like a flint* and moving through death into life.

The faith of the men and women of the Bible was a faith with backbone and perseverance, which trusted and hoped in God, regardless of the circumstances: 'Now faith is the substance of things hoped for, the evidence of things not seen' (Hebrews 11:1 KJV). This was a persistent belief that God could give life to dead things. At some point in our lives we will have to hope against hope, we will have to believe for meaning and wholeness when there is nothing but broken pieces lying around our feet.

God does his best work with our brokenness. Brokenness and dis-appointment are not the end. Wondrously, it is where God specializes. Hope and brokenness are bound up together in mysterious grace, because ultimately our hope is sourced in a Person – the hope of the world, who walked right into the hopelessness of our lives. The hope of the world is the God who suffered, even unto death.

God is *close* to the broken-hearted. We witness this truth as a recurring theme throughout the ancient scriptures: God drawn to brokenness and emptiness, in creation, in the life of the patriarchs, with the Hebrew slaves, in Israel's sojourn right through to the time of exile, and we see it ultimately personified in the person of Jesus. The Messiah was both the suffering servant and the hope of all glory. As Alan Scott has said, 'the two exist dynamically and inseparably in him'. Only in God can these two exist without being mutually exclusive. The encouragement then is to 'come boldly' before God in these times for help and comfort. We can *lean into* God even as we process the pain, we can be true to the reality of our suffering and pursue hope in equal measure. We don't have to be limited to the size of our wounds for the 'outcome of kingdom suffering is irreversible hope, enduring hope, life-giving hope'.[12] This is the subversive truth we embody as followers of Jesus in this world.

A SPACIOUS PLACE –
EVERYTHING IS SPIRITUAL

Hope had been deferred for a season of my life, but desire was rising inside me again. Glimmers of hope gave way to moments of planning and possibility for the future. Psalm 18 had provided me with the soul language I needed in my darkest of days, but now, further into the Psalm, I was finding new language to articulate the potential of a hopeful future:

---

[12] Alan Scott, via Twitter, https://twitter.com/Alan_Scott.

> He sent from on high, he took me;
> he drew me out of many waters.
> He rescued me from my strong enemy
> and from those who hated me,
> for they were too mighty for me.
> They confronted me in the day of my calamity,
> but the LORD was my support.
> He brought me out into a broad place;
> he rescued me, because he delighted in me.
>
> Psalm 18:16–19

As the days went by, hope was drip-fed into the sickness of my heart and I slowly became aware that the place of reorientation, the 'spacious place' I was being invited into, involved a corresponding decision from me. It was a decision to step over a threshold, to walk into the new. We choose and declare hope before we are fully in it, I was learning. Adversity was becoming the birthplace for renewal and life, brokenness the opportunity for a deeper wholeness than I had ever known. Hope didn't come as a 'Damascus road' encounter. Rather, like glimmers of light glancing through the gaps in the curtains at dawn, hope appeared tenderly and subtly. In gentle but profound ways I was becoming aware of an innate sacredness to simply being alive I hadn't experienced before. I was discovering, with the help of Frederick Buechner, that 'either life is holy with meaning, or life doesn't mean a damn thing'.[13] The rebirth of my whole inward man was taking place and the world was laden with fresh wonder. My life was awakened to holy moments in the midst of the humdrum of everyday life as I recognized a new sanctity in people and places where I never had before. C.S. Lewis again helped to confirm my gentle and gradual reawakening:

> There was no sudden, striking or emotional transition. Like the warming of a room or the coming of daylight. When you first notice them they have already been going on for some time.[14]

---

[13] Frederick Buechner, *Secrets in the Dark: A Life in Sermons*, Bravo Ltd, new edition (3 January 2007).

[14] C.S. Lewis, *A Grief Observed*.

In the earthy reality of my experience of death and resurrection I was learning that life itself is an epiphany. I felt like a newborn baby at times, only in an adult's body, possessing developed senses and faculties that allowed me to contemplate the magnificence of a new world more fully and with new-found wonder. Understanding the fundamental essence of life as a pure and untainted gift aided my revelation that what was happening inside me was the beginning of *resurrection*. The first glimmers of light were waking up the night of Holy Saturday. Easter Sunday's arrival was imminent, and 'God shall help her, just at the break of dawn' (Psalm 46:5 NKJV). I was alive again and as the great ragamuffin Brennan Manning reminded me: 'all is grace'.[15]

In resurrection, hope is alive and holiness is everywhere; the sound of music, the taste of coffee, the beauty of creation, the eyes of a friend. As I allowed myself to live *into* these moments I began to realize that holiness is all around me. The subconscious religious lines that formed boundaries around my previous worldview, dividing sacred and secular, had disappeared in my 'death' and I was seeing traces of the divine everywhere.

A year after Lindsay died I wrote these words in my journal, as the first shoots of life broke through in my heart and I saw the first glimmers of light moving towards me from the far end of the tunnel. Hope had arrived.

In this week of deep sorrow, I also want to acknowledge this … I am still standing. If I am honest I have a fear that maybe people assume because I am through a year, I should be back to normal soon. Of course, it is not like that at all. At the same time though I realize that I have

---

[15] Brennan Manning's autobiography, *All is Grace: A Ragamuffin Memoir*, David C. Cook (4 October 2011).

made it through the year. Sometimes I have not wanted to stand but God in his grace has picked me up each time I have fallen. I want to acknowledge that in the midst of the pain and suffering I have touched parts of the goodness and love of God that have been deeply profound. I am learning all the time about suffering, most of which I cannot really put into words, but I know in some strange, mysterious way I have found God there. I have found a God who, though often in silence, suffers with me and for me. I have found that he feels my pain and has even taken it into himself. I have found that God is Jesus with the scars. I am finding that when I choose to be true to my pain, and allow God to touch it in its rawest state, little shoots of life begin to slowly grow. This new life, as early and as fragile as it still is, has discovered that holiness is all around us and that truth is to be found not in tagging a few scriptures onto the end of abstract sentences but in being true to the experience of the gift of life given to us by our Maker, allowing his Spirit to lead us to his love. So if we engage with the suffering that life will inevitably bring us all, I think we understand more of God and if we choose to, love more like him. So in the midst of unanswered questions, searing pain, and deep sorrow, I give thanks to God that in his grace he gave me the privilege of being loved by and loving, a princess. I thank him that I have suffered so deeply because he gave me the joy of loving so fully. And I thank him for not leaving me alone in the suffering but rather in allowing me to wrestle with him, he allowed me to touch him.

CHAPTER TEN

TRANSFORMATION

There are those who suffer wounds themselves but bring others the medicine that restores health.[1]

Gregory the Great

Life can only be understood backwards; but it must be lived forwards.

Sören Kierkegaard

GIVE IT AWAY SON, WE GIVE THIS LOVE AWAY

Fourteen months after Lindsay's death, lying on a bed in a hotel room in Ibiza, I had a eureka moment. I was back in San Antonio with Brian, helping with the work of 24-7 Ibiza. I was resting, escaping from the hot Mediterranean sun and preparing for a night on the streets with the 24-7 Ibiza team. Outside, West End anthems were pumping through the streets and the sound of effervescent young holidaymakers filled the skies. I lay reflecting on my own journey and pondering the culture around me – so many young, carefree spirits hungry for love

---

[1] Gregory the Great, via Renovaré.

and prepared to do anything for it. They were living the dream but the streets were filled with broken and lonely hearts. I leafed through my Bible and my eyes locked on to words from Paul's letter to the Corinthian church, and as I read them the world seemed to stand still. I had read these verses many times before but here, in this moment, it felt like the words on the page magnified before my eyes, moving slowly towards me.

> Praise be to the God and Father of our Lord Jesus Christ, the Father of compassion and the God of all comfort, who comforts us in all our troubles, so that we can comfort those in any trouble with the comfort we ourselves have received from God. For just as the sufferings of Christ flow over into our lives, so also through Christ our comfort overflows. *If we are distressed, it is for your comfort and salvation; if we are comforted, it is for your comfort,* which produces in you patient endurance of the same sufferings we suffer.
>
> 2 Corinthians 1:3–6, NIV 1984; italics mine

I wrote these thoughts in my journal:

> When I was a young Christian, I was really inspired by these verses, sharing God's comfort with the world. Like most other scriptures, they have taken on a much deeper meaning in the new paradigm I am now living my life in. I am guessing that Paul, when explaining the 'comfort' we can offer to the world, was not referring to the warm fuzzy feeling we get when we are young in our faith but rather an overflow of the comfort we have received from God in the midst of the furnace of great suffering. We all have experienced some level of brokenness in our lives and we will continue to. As followers of Jesus we have been called out of the darkness of the world but we should never forget our identification with those outside of Christ ... we are all part of a broken humanity. The beauty of the commission of Jesus to 'go

into all the world' is that the healing (comfort) we have received from wrestling with the great Presence in our times of deepest need naturally compels us to carry this comfort to our hurting and broken fellow human beings ... *'just as the sufferings of Christ flow over into our lives, so also through Christ our comfort overflows'.* Paul seems to have got to the place of spiritual maturity where he could actually understand the missional motive in suffering and trials; he embraced his trials knowing that in doing so others could be comforted, healed and restored: *'if we are distressed, it is for your comfort and salvation; if we are comforted, it is for your comfort, which produces in you patient endurance of the same sufferings we suffer.'* Surely this is the mark of those great in the kingdom. God of all comfort helps us through the honesty of our suffering not to withdraw and become bitter but to allow our experience of the tribulations of life to contribute to the extension of your kingdom through an overflow of your love, healing and presence that has infiltrated the deepest places of our souls.

These verses and the spirit behind them gripped my whole being – it was as if revelation illuminated my soul. Paul was providing the most radical example of a life that looks like the *kenosis* of Jesus. His spiritual maturity reveals not only a profound selfless endurance in suffering but a clear reflection of the Christ who 'emptied himself' (Philippians 2:7). Paul learned how to 'rejoice in suffering', for he knew that the comfort he received from God in these difficult seasons could overflow into the broken hearts of humanity all around him. This was life fully immersed in the Father's heart.

In chapter two, I mentioned the song lyric that haunted me for days after Lindsay's death, 'where does the love go now?' Fourteen months later I found a redemptive answer in the words of Paul to the Corinthians. I heard the Father whisper what have become touchstone words for me: 'Give it away, son, we give this love away.'

In that moment these words were imprinted on my heart as the recalibrated mission statement of my life. I had received an avalanche of the healing balm of God; I had encountered a depth of love and measure of his comfort *I would not have known without this experience of loss.* I now understood that this was for much more than my own desperate need of healing – in the redemptive economy of God this love would overflow for the consolation of broken people all around me.

'Give it away, son, we give this love away.'

RESOLVING GRIEF

It was Elisabeth Kübler-Ross who first defined the now-familiar five stages of grief.[2] Denial. Anger. Bargaining. Depression. Acceptance. Counsellors, pastors and social workers are skilled in the art of moving people through these stages. The final one is acceptance. Acceptance is the difficult, yet important, place one is encouraged to reach. At this point, survivors are encouraged to bring closure to their season of mourning and to face the inevitable future without their past partner, dream or ideal. They do this by developing a calm retrospective view and a stabilization of emotions. While this 'final' stage was important for me to embrace, I came to realize that, on its own, it wouldn't be enough. Acceptance may help us to acknowledge the past, but it does little to help us face the future without a 'second-best' mentality.

When I chatted these thoughts through with Andrea she told me about another stage in the grief process, a place beyond acceptance, a place not everyone attains. Andrea described this final stage: *resolving grief.* At first I didn't like the sound of *resolving* anything. It sounded too clinical, too neat and tidy. It conjured sterile images of

---

[2] Elisabeth Kübler-Ross, *On Death and Dying*, Routledge (29 August 2008).

squaring everything off in a classroom by coming to an agreed solution, tying up the 'loose ends' and closing off all the still fragile emotions and unanswered questions. My luminous darkness had taught me that there was too much mystery, too much holy nuance, bound up in suffering for it to be neatly solved. So she needed to convince me.

When Andrea explained further, I began to feel intrigued. She described how it was possible for the individual walking through the stages of grief and loss to eventually begin to lift their gaze out of the agony of their own soul and look *redemptively* into the world around them. In doing so, they experience renewed purpose and meaning in life. The once-perceived inexorable nature of loss can be reversed, leading to an overflow of empathy, goodness and comfort in the lives of others. In that hotel room in Ibiza, I knew this was what my epiphany was all about.

> 'Give it away son, we give this love away.'

There is something about the process of passing from life into death, and then, from death into life that is inscribed onto every human heart. Meaning found in suffering, light emerging out of darkness, hope conquering despair, this is the essence of flourishing humanity on this earth. This is where we are transformed into something more like our true selves. Nicholas Wolterstorff, who tragically lost his son in a mountain climbing accident, describes the disguised grace found in suffering better than anyone:

> And sometimes when the cry is intense, there emerges a radiance which elsewhere seldom appears: a glow of courage, of love, of insight, of selflessness, of faith. In that radiance we see best what humanity was meant to be ... In the valley of suffering, despair and bitterness are brewed. But there also character is made. The valley of suffering is the vale of soul-making.[3]

There are layers of sacred significance to be found in our suffering,

---

[3] Nicholas Wolterstorff, *Lament for a Son*, Eerdmans (31 December 1996) via Jerry Sittser, *A Grace Disguised: How the Soul Grows Through Loss*, Zondervan, enlarged edition (1 December 2004).

not in some contrived-existentialist-coffee-shop-conversation kind of way, but in real and tangible ways the healing balm of the Father can overflow out from within us into the brokenness of humanity. My story, I was beginning to realize, was aligning itself with the words of Barbara Brown Taylor, 'the testimony of those who have come through the dark, they would not have chosen it, but they would not give it back'.[4]

LIGHT FOR ALL

In the opening pages of this book I described Lindsay's and my love for Africa and in particular our connection with the people of Jandira, Uganda. During those special days in July 2006, we knew we were being drawn into something that was far beyond a two-week summer-mission trip. We couldn't know how our relationship would unfold with the people of this small village in the middle of the African bush, but we were pretty sure our lives were being woven into this community for the long term. A distinct, albeit far-fetched dream Lindsay and I carried home from that first trip was to build a secondary school in Jandira. We had listened to Pastor Richard's desire to build upon the strong foundation these children had received through the primary school he had pioneered and we imagined the privilege it would be to help these poverty-stricken young people right through their education, in a loving environment committed to their holistic development. It would be a school and a community we could continue to support and visit over the forthcoming years, leading our church community into lasting friendships and relationships with these young people, finding ways to unlock the God-given potential they all possessed! We knew it could be achieved but we suspected it would take years to plan and do.

A few months after Lindsay's death, I was at a youth festival in Belfast, 'Summer Madness', overseeing some of the young people from

---

[4] Barbara Brown Taylor, source unknown.

our church who were attending. I found myself wandering around the camp oblivious to much of what was going on, thinking about Lindsay and reminiscing about our time in Africa. I don't know if you have ever had one of those moments where it seems like the world stands still and a glimpse of what seems like your future collides with your present. That day I peered into the future and instinctively made the decision that our dream would become a reality. We would just do it. We would build that secondary school in Lindsay's memory. And as I grieved her loss I would throw my heart and soul into making this happen. Not in ten years' time, not in five years' time, as we had previously thought. We would start now. I texted my friend John, my co-conspirator and our fellow leader on the first trip I took to Africa. He replied immediately: 'let's do it.' It was at best naïve and more likely impossible. We shared the dream with family, friends and our church family – everyone was in!

My mother and sister held a fundraising night on my brother-in-law Ricky's birthday. Guests were invited to donate towards the purchase of land on which the school would be built instead of buying birthday presents. We reckoned that we needed £10,000 to buy a particular plot of land and hoped that the evening would get us off to a good start. Incredibly, we raised £23,000! The generosity of those who came along exceeded our imaginations. The project was a goer.

Early in 2008 I traveled to Uganda, with our friend Grant, and visited Jandira to purchase the land. It was my first visit since Lindsay and I had spent our summer there eighteen months earlier. It was the most sad and beautiful trip I have ever been on, and is probably best summarized in the blog entry I wrote at the time.

> We arrived on Sunday night and it is great to be back in Africa. I love the smell of this place ... you sense it as you walk off the plane. I love it ... it really is home from home here ... I always find myself more chilled here, more true to myself, more aware of God and it is here I find the deepest insights to myself and life.
>
> Of course, though, it is bittersweet. It is my first time back in Africa without Lins. It was the home of both our

souls and at times I am so aware of her absence. Today I went back to Source of Light primary school where we spent a month in July 06 and made many friends. It was amazing, strange, beautiful and sad, all in one, being there today. The children sang for us and reminded us of their love for us.

It is hard not to think from time to time Lins should be here. And it is easy for the questions to start rising again ... all the questions that suggest there is no sense in what has happened ... I could start to tell you what those questions are but I will not. There is no need and I have learned that coming through grief (if this is even the right phrase) is all about choice. It is about choosing to believe that, in the midst of the brokenness of life, there is a God who weeps with us, and, in his power and mercy, redeems the most hopeless of cases.

As the questions stir within me again, I realize here in Africa, that I have actually found a deeper place. A place I can go to in my soul beneath the questions that want to rise to the surface ... in the midst of the sadness I have found a place deeper than the place of confusion and questions. It is the deepest part of me, a place that is scarred with pain but a place I am learning is full and satisfied and alive ... alive again ... I am realizing that I have experienced something that was a deep and holy privilege. So I choose to try and live from this place ... a place where I realize the deep privilege it was to have loved Lindsay, to have won her heart, to have shared life with her, to have come to Africa with her, to have realized dreams together, to have been blown by the Wind of God with her, to love her through her sickness and to have experienced grace and true beauty through her, especially in how she handled her suffering. And I choose to believe, as difficult as it is (and even though my emotions are telling me the opposite), God has not finished with me yet ... that my story is not over and that new chapters have to be written … that nothing will be the same again but yet there is hope of a future. One of those chapters includes journey our friends In building a secondary school in her memory. Many of the kids here don't have a chance of secondary school education and Lins was passionate about ways of developing people and communities in the poorer regions of the world.

Grant and I visited the site today. It sits on the top of a hill and overlooks the whole region. It is a brilliant and beautiful view. When Lins was sick my mum felt God say, Lindsay's life would be a 'light to the nations'. Obviously Mum, like us all, hoped and prayed this meant something other than what has transpired. Through the hell of these past months Mum has held on to that verse though and today I was reminded about it as I stood on that hill and looked all around me, praying and believing that Lins's life, which has inspired us to build this school, will be a light to the nations. That the young people here she was passionate about will be not just be well educated, but will come to know Jesus and his good news message for the world and that through them many will be drawn to the Great Light of the World.

I dream of a day when this place is established as a Christ-centred school, committed to training and developing young people who will affect society at all different levels, influencing the country of Uganda, the region of East Africa, the whole of this beautiful continent and the rest of the world with the Jesus-message … the message of the kingdom of heaven which comes to earth …

Pastor Richard, who will be the headmaster, wants to call this school, 'Light to the Nations Secondary School', and no matter what, we are going to build this thing!

And build it we did. Later in the summer of that year, eighty people from our church went out to Uganda and we started to construct the school. A few months before, I had stood on this incredible site, a hilltop with the most spectacular view of the African bush, overlooking little villages dotted throughout the landscape. I imagined children coming up to this 'city on a hill' – a place of refuge, learning, development and love – and leaving it empowered by the message of the kingdom of God. As we laid the first bricks I became aware that this dream was becoming a reality and I was in this for life. The cement that held the bricks together became a metaphor for the holy commitment that would bind my heart to these Ugandan children for the rest of my life. I could never simply build a few classrooms and walk away. My life would be entwined with this village and with these people forever. I was daunted by the commitment this would involve. Yet this emotion was surpassed by the privilege it felt to know, serve and live alongside these children for the long haul. The school opened in January 2009 with over fifty students. At the time of writing, around a thousand students have passed through the school, gaining a recognized education and being nurtured in a culture founded on the kingdom of God.

Many of the pupils of Light for All secondary were young children during Lindsay's first trip. Children who had sat on Lindsay's knees, playing and laughing with her, braiding her hair and stroking her white 'Mzungu' skin, despite the fact they were evidently malnourished, poorly dressed and, only through Pastor Richard's dedication to the primary school, just beginning to gain an education. They have grown up into the most outstanding young men and women. One of these boys is called William. On our first visit in 2006 William was only nine. He was shy, but friendly, with a beautiful innocent smile. He was an orphan and Pastor Richard had adopted him as his own, along with a number of other children, children who had slept on mattresses squashed into every last inch of floor in his home. William, like many of the boys there, loved to play football with us. He helped us build, wheeling the wheelbarrow and carrying bricks, and we would make sure he stood beside us in church, smiling joyfully as we worshipped God together. Over the years, as William attended Light for All Secondary School, he has grown into a strong young man and leader. He recently sent me an email telling me that he has begun a project in the prisons where he and some fellow students visit inmates offering prayer, counseling and fellowship. They also travel to surrounding villages praying for the sick and the disabled, running programs to care for other orphans and visiting the elderly. William is just one of the students who is a living fulfillment of the legacy of Lindsay's life and the vision of the Light for All Secondary School.

TRANSFORMED IN LOVE AND FOR LOVE

Each time I go back to Uganda to visit the students of Light for All and the people of Jandira, I hear that whisper, 'Give it away son, we give this love away', and I think of 2 Corinthians 1:5, 6 (NIV 1984).

> For just as the sufferings of Christ flow over into our lives, so also through Christ our comfort overflows. If we are distressed, it is for your comfort and salvation; if we are comforted, it is for your comfort.

I am humbled at how God has allowed the experience of his beautiful comfort, poured into my heart, to overflow into the lives of these children in Jandira, and how in his mysterious grace-filled ways he has allowed the legacy of Lindsay's life, one of complete trust and dependency on him, to be lived on in the lives of these children.

I had wrestled with God and been wounded in the deepest part of my being. But I met him, face to face, and now, like Jacob, I was limping forward with a new name. I had surrendered to the mystery of his sovereignty and in doing so enveloped myself in his awesome character. Like Job, I had initially cursed the day I was born, but Job's relentless perseverance also inspired me to hang on, knowing that while we don't always get an explanation for our suffering, we do get God himself, and when we do, he is more than enough. I learned to trust in goodness beyond that which my limited reasoning could comprehend. I have lived the truth that Lindsay's life and mine have been woven into a wider and richer, enhanced and ennobled story. To the secularist and atheist, this hope of the Christian is inconceivable and stupefying – our lives hung out on the promise that the suffering of this present world can't be compared to the glory that will one day be revealed in us.

The revelation of sovereign grace in this luminous darkness allowed me to let go of the mechanical god of hyper-Calvinism I had grown up with, the same god many of 'Job's comforters' seemed to know, as they sought to bring comfort to my grief. This worldview infers a God who deliberately predestined this horror in my life, as a pious test of faith, to see if I would make the grade. This view has become abhorrent to me and I have realized it is inconsistent with the Abba revealed to us in Jesus. Tozer was right: 'What comes into our minds when we think about God is the most important thing about us.'[5] Walking prayerfully through suffering purifies our perception and focuses the lens more sharply on the face of Jesus. God knew that Lindsay would die and for reasons beyond me chose not to intervene in the ways I had wanted him to, yet I had put my hope in a God, who, when Lindsay died, was, I believe, the first to cry, feeling every emotion that seared my heart. Leaning into the mystery of God allowed me to fall into him, into Love Himself and in doing so let Love transform me.

> God does not cause suffering. God suffers suffering. Those who walk the road which leads to God participate in it as surely as a cheap hotel has bed bugs. To resist suffering is to cripple the spirit as well as the body. To roll with it does not lesson the pain, but makes of suffering a teacher, unwelcome yet formative. Those who have had their hearts gouged by suffering find that it provides a channel for a deep river to flow. Though the sun does not shine in the valley, it is still there … if the valleys of Godzone are dark and frightening, they are as full of God as every other part of the road. Those traveling through them come out stronger and surer and more able to love without fear. They belong now to the fellowship of the suffering, and will recognize others who have endured the valleys by something in their eyes. They will not say more than one or two words about it, but they will share a secret knowledge.[6]

---

[5] A.W. Tozer, *The Knowledge of the Holy*, HarperOne (6 October 2009).
[6] Mike Riddell, *Godzone: A Traveller's Guide*, Lion Books (June 2000).

Mike Riddell's words capture it beautifully: 'Those who have had their hearts gouged by suffering find that it provides a channel for a deep river to flow.' God hadn't minimized or trivialized my pain – he had suffered it with me, yet he, because of his love and his victory over suffering, was transforming me *in* love and *for* love from the inside out! God wasn't a schoolteacher waiting to see if I had simply passed the test, or a policeman making sure I had obeyed all the rules. He was a Father who had stepped into my pain, carried it and gave me the radiance of his face to light up my darkness. Faith and hope were crucial virtues to exercise on my healing journey but renewed wholeness would be completed only by the greatest of them all – love. Faith and hope had pulled my soul into a new place of perspective, allowing me to imagine new possibilities and see a new horizon. But it was the unrelenting love of the Triune God that ensured the 'threefold cord [faith, hope and love] was not quickly broken'. It was the loving delight of the Father, deeper than any other emotion, constant and steadfast, that allowed me to even contemplate hope; the gentle but firm friendship of Jesus gently rising faith within me to believe I could live again, that *all of me* could live again; and the soothing comfort of the Holy Spirit warming up my shriveled soul with life. It was love that ultimately transformed me through my suffering, creating something new, enlarging my heart in compassion and expanding me in impossibility and wonder. The Psalmist knew it only too well:

> he rescued me, because he delighted in me …
> your right hand supported me,
> and your gentleness made me great.
> Psalm 18:19, 35

Lindsay and I had 'tasted and seen that God was good' in loving one another 'till death do you part'. But now something even more profound had taken place within me through the longer arduous walk of love, loss and subsequent healing. A deep deposit of the Father's heart was sewn into the very fabric of my soul inscribing itself on my heart and he was teaching me how to allow this love to overflow out of me. Viktor Frankl has words much more articulate than mine:

> Then I grasped the meaning of the greatest secret that human poetry and human thought and belief have to impart: The salvation of Man is through love and in love. I understood how a man who has nothing left in this world still may know bliss, be it only for a brief moment, in the contemplation of his beloved. In a position of utter desolation, when Man cannot express himself in positive action, when his only achievement may consist in enduring his sufferings in the right way – an honourable way – in such a position Man can, through loving contemplation of the image he carries of his beloved, achieve fulfillment. For the first time in my life, I was able to understand the meaning of the words, 'The angels are lost in perpetual contemplation of an infinite glory.'[7]

DEEP GRATITUDE: A CHANGE IN PERSPECTIVE

This search for meaning through the resolution of my grief brought with it a shift in outlook. The days spent honestly leaning into the pain of uncomfortable questions and protest at God started to give way to new patterns of thought. A change of perspective gradually happened inside of me. My early conclusions, detailed in my days of protest, had brought me to an apparent impasse in my relationship with God:

> God had robbed me of something I felt I had deserved.
> I had been given a raw deal.
> He hadn't fulfilled his side of the exchange.
> I honoured him and he hadn't come through for me in return.

---

[7] Viktor Frankl, *Man's Search for Meaning*, Beacon Press, 1st edition (1 June 2006).

> I had been short-changed – I had been given twenty
> months of marriage with the woman I had waited for
> my whole life.

Now, though, I started to see things differently. Walking into and through the darkest part of the grief-tunnel, clinging onto his presence through the wrestle, not letting him go until he blessed me had been the place of luminosity. He had delicately unravelled the nexus of my soul, broadening my horizons, widening my perspective.

I was taken back to when as an aimless 17-year-old I was found out by the love of Jesus. In response to encountering his love, I completely yielded all that I was to him and I lovingly offered him my whole heart, asking him to take it and do with it what he wanted, for I knew he alone could be trusted with it. I told him I would do whatever he wanted me to do and go wherever he wanted me to go. My bridges were burned. I was exhilarated by newfound purpose and the adventure that lay ahead. For the ten years that followed my teenage prayer of surrender, I had been under the impression that the way I was fulfilling this vow was through my 'ministry' – leading a church, preaching his word, leading mission teams, changing the world! Slowly though, and inconspicuously at first, I found myself contemplating another way God had allowed me to fulfill this vow. What if part of the outworking of these promises I had wholeheartedly made to God involved, more than anything else, loving Lindsay – involved loving her unto death? What if loving Lindsay was less about her 'partnering with me in ministry' and more about me walking with her and carrying her, literally, through a brutal sickness? What if God allowed *me* to be the one who would love a girl that was going to die when she was 23? What if God, in his lavish kindness, in the midst of this broken world he weeps over, wanted Lindsay to experience a completeness of love and oneness on this earth before she would know it fully in paradise with him? And what if the way God weaved my naïve but wholly genuine surrendered life into Lindsay's was for this very purpose?

As these thoughts took shape in my heart and mind I found myself speechless before the Father. My present categories of faith were no match for such wonder and awe. Certain questions have remained unanswered about why Lindsay died so young, but there was a much stronger emotion rising inside me. For someone comprehending loss it was, counter-intuitively, the emotion of *gratitude*. Anger and rage had subsided and I found my way into a new normal – a state of gratefulness that was shaping my soul. I was grateful to God for allowing me to be Lindsay's husband. My heart discovered a way to trump any sentimental self-pitying for I was aware of the astonishing privilege it was to be 'chosen' by God for such a purpose. Chosen to *complete* Lindsay, chosen to love her like Jesus did and reciprocally, chosen to experience in my own life such a sacred love. It was the essence of paradoxical truth again – the strange but liberating sensation of life in all its fullness. In God's mysterious and wondrous grace-filled ways, he had woven our lives together so we could enjoy something of heaven before the pain of this time-bound earth would sever our connection. I could not have comprehended all of this at Lindsay's death nor could I have accepted it, but in retrospect, I am not sure I would want to change it. As Brueggemann concludes:

> We do not always know the gifts of God in advance. But given a perspective of faith we can in subsequent reflection discern the amazing movement of God in events we had not noticed or even assigned to other causes.[8]

No matter the magnitude of our loss or intensity of our pain, if we are 'in Christ' there is always a new opportunity available. There is an incorruptible seed planted in the deepest parts of us that death itself cannot destroy. The most spectacular metamorphosis in all of creation occurs when the image bearers of the Creator present their broken hearts to the *God of all comfort*, hang onto him through the greatest suffering and wait for new life to break through.

---

[8] Walter Brueggemann, *Genesis: Interpretation: A Bible Commentary for Teaching and Preaching*, Westminster John Knox Press, 1st edition (25 January 2010).

THE BATTLE OF LOVE

The lesson of my luminous darkness is therefore: *there is a beautiful mysterious sacredness to be encountered in our woundedness.* God seems to be able to use our pain in ways that he can't use our strengths. There is something about our brokenness and vulnerability that identifies with humanity more naturally and authentically than our impressive qualities can. Most people can't relate to your excellence but they can relate to your brokenness. As C.S. Lewis is often quoted '… pain insists upon being attended to. God whispers to us in our pleasures, speaks in our conscience, but shouts in our pains: it is his megaphone to rouse a deaf world.'[9] This was never more impressed upon me than when I heard Brennan Manning emotionally give tribute to the genius and beauty of Rich Mullins after his tragic death. I always find the following transcript incredibly moving.

> There's a scene in Thornton Wilder's play *The Angel that Troubled the Waters* which to me really captures the essence of the life and the spirituality of Rich Mullins.
>
> The scene is a doctor comes to the pool everyday wanting to be healed of his melancholy and his gloom and his sadness. Finally, the angel appears. The doctor, he's a medical doctor, goes to step into the water. The angel blocks his entrance and says, 'No, step back, the healing is not for you.' The doctor pleads, 'But I've got to get into the water. I can't live this way.' The angel says, 'No, this moment is not for you.' And he says, 'But how can I live this way?'
>
> The angel says to him, 'Doctor, without your wounds where would your power be? It is your melancholy that makes your low voice tremble into the hearts of men and women. The very angels themselves cannot persuade the wretched and blundering children of this earth as can one human being broken on the wheels of living. In love's service, only wounded soldiers can serve.'
>
> And to me the theme of that story is the theme to Rich Mullins's life. All grace, all light, all truth, all power is communicated through

---

[9] C.S. Lewis, *The Problem of Pain.*

the vulnerability, the brokenness, the utter honesty of men and women who have been shipwrecked, heartbroken, broken in the wheels of living. In love's service, only wounded soldiers can serve. And to me, the power of Rich Mullins's life lay in the power of his brokenness, the power in his unblinking honesty, his deeply moving sincerity and God, I miss him.[10]

I have never forgotten this majestic line, 'in the battle of love only wounded soldiers can serve'. This is the kingdom way: those broken, busted and heartbroken, have not only received the good news that the Kingdom is near but have been called as those best positioned to serve in the ongoing mission of Jesus. For somehow emptied of ourselves, the defensive wall of invulnerability broken down around us, we are now prime targets for the extravagant grace of Jesus and the lavish love of the Father. As the Holy Spirit pours his love into our hearts it floods our beings, healing our hearts and inebriating our senses in such a liberating way that it overflows from us into our fellow humanity.

The path I had journeyed wasn't enjoyable in the common use of the word. And it certainly wasn't the course, given the choice, I would have picked for my life before Lindsay's sickness and death. But I have been transformed and know a wholeness I never imagined was possible. God did something, in the midst of my tragic circumstances, that was greater, much greater than I. His glory increased, my character deepened, his purposes unfolded. If I hadn't experienced it and come through it I wouldn't be the same perfectly loved, totally dependent and trusting son that I am now. For in the battle of love, only wounded soldiers can fight.

Where does the love go now Father?
Give it away son, give _my_ love away.

Oh, the depth of the riches of the wisdom and knowledge of God!

---

[10] This is a transcript from Brennan Manning's tribute to Rich Mullins in the film _Homeless Man – The Restless Heart of Rich Mullins_, directed by Ben Pearson. USA: Compassion International/Myrrh Records, 1998.

How unsearchable his judgments, and his paths beyond
tracing out!
To him be the glory forever!

Romans 11:33, 36B NIV

It is well with my soul.

EPILOGUE:
RESURRECTION

Resurrection means the last thing is never the final thing.

Buechner

One Sunday night in winter 2008, I saw Rachel. I was hovering at the edges of a pre-gathering coffee at a church in Belfast when a striking dark-haired beauty weaved her way through the young adults chatting enthusiastically. I felt like I knew her, or I would know her, or somehow was already known by her. After the service, I noticed my friend Owen talking to her. This seemed the perfect opportunity to catch up with Owen! He started to introduce us. 'I'm Rachel', she said, and then ever-so-gently drew me into the conversation. Owen was relegated to the role of spectator as the three-way conversation quickly became two-way. He lingered just long enough to encourage Rachel to take my details – he knew what he was doing!

I walked towards the car that night trying not to get ahead of myself. I cautioned myself: the ten-minute conversation was no different to any of the exchanges I'd had with girls in the previous few months. Rachel just happened to be in the 'stunning' category, which is what made it harder for me to forget about her.

Hope, as I described in chapter nine, is dangerous – something I needed to be careful about. And what would a beautiful and free-spirited girl like Rachel really want with someone with issues and history, like me? But I couldn't ignore the chemistry I sensed in our brief encounter; couldn't stifle the thoughts about her racing around my mind. To my surprise and delight, Rachel emailed me the next night, and I asked her to join me for a drink the following week.

RADICAL MIDDLE

A few months before, I had talked with Andrea about the possibility of meeting someone again. She injected hope into my nervous and tentative outlook by introducing me to an intriguing possibility, a potential encounter she described as 'the radical middle'. She explained that, often in God's beautiful redemptive purposes and exquisite timing, there can be a 'place of meeting', a transcendental connection. If I began to journey towards the 'radical middle' there was a very real possibility, in the providence of God, that without my knowing, someone could be moving towards me. This place of meeting, this radical middle, she promised, would be risky but potentially magical. She encouraged me to lean my heart into this new place, fix my gaze towards it and move my whole being in that direction. As Andrea shared testimonies of others who had experienced such a healing, I was in equal and opposite ways encouraged and skeptical, judging the whole idea as fanciful thinking at best. With nothing else to lose, I decided to trust her and gently tip-toed forward. If I reflected for too long on the 'what-might-be', an overwhelming nausea, not unlike that on your first day of school, would rise up inside me. How does a 27-year-old widower beleaguered with grief go about chatting to a girl, let alone begin a relationship?

As I drove to Rachel's house after my football training that cold wet Tuesday night, just over a week since we had met, I felt exposed, a ball of nerves. I wasn't really sure what I should do, how I should act, what I should say (or not say)! I had lost my confidence. As we chatted I was full of nervous apprehension, but also bubbling with excitement.

Rachel, on the other hand, was pure class. Her sublime poise and natural grace did what I thought was impossible – she captivated my heart all over again. It was never going to be easy to love someone who had been through what I had. She handled it with a dignity, gentleness and compassion that made me fall for her even more. Rachel possessed the most exceptional and uncanny intuition which meant she effortlessly understood the delicate balance required as we began to grow in our relationship. She showed me empathy and compassion yet remained confident in her own self, her own life, her own faith. On the one hand, I needed someone to 'get me' and at least try to understand what I had been through, but on the other I needed someone to challenge me to the new, to the 'what could be'. It wasn't always easy. None of our parents, never mind our peers, had experienced anything like this and we had no textbook to guide us. Yet we found a way to work it out through rugged commitment and honest conversation, finding our way towards oneness. Rachel's sparkling intrigue drew me towards her, stimulating my heart to believe that the days ahead no longer had to be second-best. Instead I was opening a new and exciting chapter of life. Rachel's fun-loving, adventurous and mature personality, without forcing anything, gently propelled me towards a hopeful future. Within eight months we were engaged, and a year later we were married.

Five years on, God has blessed us with two adorable daughters – Annie and Erin. They are sheer joy. I know a fullness of life greater than I could ever have imagined. As Rachel's soul has been joined with my own I have experienced a renewed completeness in my life that has healed my past, granted me a new space to enjoy the present, and gifted me a new permission to gaze forwards. Life is full and wonderful and I am still alive – more alive than ever.

PLACE OF ABUNDANCE

My luminous darkness experience, wrestling with love through the dark night of the soul, has helped me 'put away my childish thinking'. God *still* brings beauty out of ashes, he is *still* making all things beautiful, he is *still* working all things together for good. My faith was tested to the point of destruction, but in assimilating the words of my faithful companions from the sacred text into my own soul, through protest and questioning and wrestling with God, my faith was refined, strengthened and enlarged. I can affirm from firsthand experience and with absolute confidence:

God is who he always said he is.

Funny that! He changes not! He is *still* the Great Shepherd who always leads his children right *through* the valley of the shadow of death. The Psalms, which had made sure I never walked alone, now gave me the language to express the unspeakable thankfulness appropriate for a new '**place of abundance**'.

> For you, God, tested us;
> you refined us like silver.
> You brought us into prison
> and laid burdens on our backs.
> You let people ride over our heads;
> we went through fire and water,
> **but you brought us to a place of abundance.**
>
> Psalm 66:10–12 NIV

MORE THAN A FAIRY TALE

It is of utmost importance that this story does not imply a kind of fairy-tale, happy-ever-after ending, which celebrates how things have worked out well for me alone.

It is important to me you hear why I wouldn't be content with that, and why I have kept this ending to the Epilogue.

Firstly, my passionate hope is that throughout these pages my story has served the purpose of drawing you into the much bigger and beautiful story of God – where all our stories are included and where all our stories find meaning. I have included, in this final chapter, how the subsequent script of my story evolved from the days of my 'dark night of the soul'. It's equally important, I feel, to be true to my present as much as I have been to my past. More simply, I thought you would like to know what happened next! But please don't allow the glow of how my life has developed to push your story into the shadows. I dearly hope you have found some healing resonance through this book. I pray it encourages you, stirring faith and breathing hope into your circumstances. But I would be so disappointed if in any way it invalidated *your* story, or the pain you are currently carrying. Resist the temptation to over-compare. *Your* story is *your* story. It is different, multi faceted and rich. Most importantly, it is of equally incalculable importance to the Father. Wherever you are right now, God believes in you. He is for you and he is with you on the messy and complex path of processing pain.

Secondly, things 'worked out for me' *not* because I deserved it. People are kind when they express thoughts like 'after all he has been through he deserves some happiness'. This, of course, is valid and the sentiment is well meaning, but the way my life has turned around, if that's what we call it, is not some form of Christian karma. Just because I might have been 'one of the good guys' who has been through hell and back, doesn't necessarily mean I am due 'the rub of the green' from God. God doesn't 'owe me one'. The goodness of God has much more to it than that. I want this book to testify to the goodness of God *beyond my circumstances*. God has been good to me because God is good. Period. Many of us know this in a head-knowledge kind of way, but the actual revelation of God's goodness has only been reinforced and strengthened through my personal luminous darkness. I can now understand God's grace through the immensity of his character, the unconditional nature of his character and the depth of his fidelity. He is always breaking up our ingrained 'karma' mentalities. Through an embrace of my loss and leaning into my pain, I have come to realize that I have been invited into a broader kaleidoscope of grace – something much more mysterious, awesome and transformational.

Thirdly, I am conscious that each of our stories follows a different trajectory. It may seem things have not turned around so sweetly for many of you as they appear to have for me. I am not naïve enough to testify: 'just hang on, it all works out in the end. Just look at me.' I watch the evening news and I am aware people are dealing with far worse things, wrestling with them, contending with painful situations around the world. As this journey has taught us, many of these tragedies require thoughtful and engaging silence, the only adequate response to such pain, rather than shallow religious hyperbole. I think about Lindsay's own beautiful family who have lost a sister, a daughter, an auntie. Nothing can ever or will ever replace her in their lives. I think of friends and my church family who have lost family members, children who have died too young, singles who have never fulfilled their dream of marriage, couples who suffer the life-long struggle of infertility, partners caring for a sick or paralyzed partner after a tragic accident or illness. Disappointment is an unwelcome but familiar experience in life. After the traumas and tragedies of life, disappointment lingers and worse can sometimes fester. Many of you, even after reading through this book, are still wondering if the cloud of unknowing and despondency will ever lift, if the gap in your soul will ever be filled again. I understand this and I hear you. Remember, in some seasons of life it's ok not to be ok. Just be true to it and pray – pray indiscriminately. Let it go through you. Processing pain calls us to the higher thinking of paradox, where we are led to hold together that wounded and wonderful holy incongruity, rather than a benign acceptance. I have found, when it comes to dealing with loss, that it is possible to be fully healed *and* for it to feel like it has never fully gone away.

Fourthly, while Rachel, Annie and Erin are signs of the ridiculous blessing of God in my life, tangible evidence of how he is able to restore to us, and a witness to his extravagant favour, I got something beyond all of these lavish gifts of God. I got something beyond all of his generous bounty.

I got him.
I got Jesus.
He gave me himself. And he is more than enough.
The risen Lord gave me himself.

This resurrection life is where I want to focus my concluding thoughts – on that hope, concrete and sure, over and above our changing circumstances and fragile world.

RESURRECTION REVISITED

Readers of this book, for the most part, will agree that beyond the excitement of chocolate inoculation at Easter, Resurrection Sunday is good reason for the church to celebrate. *Christ is risen! He is risen indeed.* The prevailing mindset of most church going believers in the western Church is something along the lines of: Jesus' resurrection completed his work on the cross, and his conquering of sin, death and hell means we can spend eternity in heaven with him. Good news, eh? Good news, yes – but there is so much more good news.

Tom Wright describes our reductionist way of comprehending the resurrection by asserting that we have replaced what the old liturgies called 'the sure and certain hope of resurrection of the dead' with 'the vague and fuzzy optimism that somehow things might work out alright in the end'. Let's clear something up. *Resurrection is not simply another sentimental way of describing passing from one world into another, and death is not the welcome companion waiting to bring us there.* Rather, our hope, despite our circumstances, is this: through Jesus' death and resurrection he has conquered sin, all its effects and consequences, overthrown the tyrant and defeated the last enemy of all, death itself. Jesus has completely vanquished the enemy. The sting has been well and truly removed. Resurrection, of which Easter is the source, means much more than Lindsay 'getting into heaven' when she died because she was 'saved'. This is only part of the truth. Lindsay, with many of our loved ones, is in paradise with Jesus. She is in a state of ecstatic, blissful union, 'with Christ which is far better'. Yet she waits with you and me and all the saints for the full consummation of God's victory, when God remakes both heaven and earth, marrying them together forever.

> Look! God's dwelling place is now among the people, and he will dwell with them. They will be his people, and God himself will be with them and be their God. 'He will wipe every tear from their eyes. There will be no more death' or

> mourning or crying or pain, for the old order of things has passed away.
>
> Revelation 21:3–4 NIV

Please don't hear this as glib or patronizing, but the great Christian hope of resurrection means, whether we experience healing instantaneously, gradually or even incompletely, it is all going to be ok in the end! The mystic Julian of Norwich famously declared: 'All shall be well, and all shall be well, and all manner of things shall be well.'

The wider horizon of this victory, this life-changing hope, this supreme act of God, is *not just stored up for us when we die, but moving towards us now*! The Hope the grave could not contain is *Hope breaking into our present context.* Tom Wright continues: 'Precisely because the resurrection has happened as an event within our own world, its implications and effects are to be felt within our world, here and now.'[1]

This, of course, was the good news Jesus proclaimed during his time on earth. His message pulsed with what seemed to be a 'too-good-to-be-true' hope – 'repent, for the kingdom of God is *among* you'. Jesus longed for humanity to know that something new was happening. Happening *now*! The king had come, and he declared an availability and demonstrability to his rule and reign breaking into our real and beaten-up everyday lives, now! This new accessibility to an atmosphere of heaven, inaugurated through the ministry of Jesus, means that resurrection hope and power are now tangibly present. 'I am the resurrection and the life' is spectacular gladness to hopeless souls. This resurrection-essence of the life and ministry of Jesus explains why he went around looking for dead things – hearts, spirits and bodies. His heavenly assignment was to restore humanity back to its original, fullness-of-life, design.

Resurrection hope is not a distant 'when the roll is called up yonder' kind of hope, it is hope hurtling towards our dying dreams and shriveled souls, *today*. The world has already been turned

---

[1] Tom Wright, *Surprised by Hope*, SPCK Publishing, 2nd edition (2011).

upside-down, that is what Easter is all about! This is what Jesus is all about.

> In this world you will have trouble. But take heart! I have overcome the world.
>
> John 16:33 NIV

This message of Jesus incarnated in his life was fulfilled through his sacrificial death and resurrection. This was a love so pure, so holy, so selfless, so powerful that the Father vindicated it by raising Jesus up from the grave. Now an irreversible shift has taken place: where sin and its grave consequences have multiplied around the world, resurrection reverses the cycle, rewriting the storyline, allowing us to lean into the future with a hope-shaped posture. One seed of resurrection life possesses the power to raise to life any area of God-given life aborted within us.

LIVING THE RESURRECTION

Resurrection is the Church's word. Appropriating Jesus' death and resurrection to our lives means that, despite our circumstances, the renewed narrative of our lives is characterized primarily by a forward momentum. We don't have to stay stuck. I can testify to that. I finally apprehended the truth that I didn't have to be rooted to my circumstances, destined to a bogged down existence in a quagmire of unrelenting grief. I began to grasp the exceptional truth that because 'the same spirit that raised Christ from the dead lives in us', I didn't have to settle for what my friend Alan Scott calls 'a theology of lack'. Disappointment, though real, would not define me. Resurrection would! No longer would I allow my understanding of God to be restricted to my disappointments. Where I once experienced death, decay and darkness, hope was inscribing rebirth, light and life on my renewed heart. It may seem at times that the stuffing has been knocked out of us so badly we are unable to even make it on to the field. I understand that. But for the most part of the game we are not on the defensive, merely holding out for a draw, extra-time and penalties. My luminous darkness has taught me that, as those who through Jesus live the resurrection, we can press in for victory, we can move forward with joyful endeavour, we can compete with resolute confidence.

We are on the front foot. We are on the winning side.

This was the central message to the early church after Jesus' ascension. It was not 'we get to go to heaven when we die', but that right now we are being 'baptised' into Christ's death and being raised up in his victorious power with the dynamic energy of his life pulsing in our hearts. As we live in the reality of this, energized by the power of his Spirit, in the prayerful posture of 'thy kingdom come on earth as it is in heaven', we are establishing beauty, truth and justice today that will be enhanced and ennobled in God's new world forever.

He is present in our suffering, yet we must remember he is still beyond us. His Spirit plunges the depths of our agonized souls, making darkness his secret place, yet he still continues to heal the sick and raise the dead. More, he asks us to do the same and even 'greater things than these'. No matter how distant it feels at the moment, my great hope for this book is that you finish it knowing that when you get Jesus, you have resurrection life pumping through your veins. We don't have to settle for the lie that the future is second best when we can know resurrection victory as a lived reality. Creation is being re-birthed in and through our surrendered hearts, serving as a signpost to the hope we will know forever. I encourage you to learn to 'live the resurrection' now, for the beautiful mystery for the Christian is, 'Christ in you the hope of glory' (Colossians 1:27).

THOMAS

All the saints have borne witness to such a God who 'calls life out of dead things'. It's no good knowing this simply in our heads, we need to encounter the reality of this in our hearts if it is to change us. The Bible character who exemplifies this is Thomas. John tells us Thomas missed seeing Jesus when he appeared to the other disciples after he rose from the dead, Thomas needed to see for himself. He declared that he wouldn't believe in Jesus' resurrection unless he could place his fingers in the holes of Jesus' nail-pierced hands and his hand in his spear-punctured side. The church subsequently has labeled him 'doubting Thomas'. Oh, the irony! I am not sure it was a 'doubting' issue for Thomas as much as it was a genuine desire to believe for himself. Christian Wiman distinguishes between 'passive doubt' and 'active doubt' – I find this helpful when thinking about Thomas. Passive doubt resigns itself to a gradual acquiescence with current circumstances which in most cases ends up in a pathetic form of self-absorbed cynicism. But active doubt is a search for something. It possesses a distinctive hunger. A hunger *for* something or someone. It is skeptical of anything false or contrived, and resists inauthentic motives; it will not settle for someone else's testimony, or live off someone else's experience. Active doubt wants to see and believe for itself and in doing so searches out something more durable, something more tangible, and something more real.

What if Thomas's doubt was *active*?

What if Thomas was carrying pain in his life, some depth of shame or disappointment that he was desperate to be free of? What if Thomas's inner voice was desperately whispering: 'If Jesus, despite the agony of his pain and death, could rise victorious over every kind of evil and darkness placed on him, maybe there is hope for the secret pain I am carrying.'

His response, when he eventually did see Jesus, is a holy, standstill moment in scripture and leaves us in no doubt that he was convinced.

> Eight days later, his disciples were inside again, and Thomas was with them. Although the doors were locked, Jesus came and stood among them and said, 'Peace be with you.' Then he said to Thomas, 'Put your finger here, and see my hands; and put out your hand, and place it in my side. Do not disbelieve, but believe.' Thomas answered him, 'My Lord and my God!'
>
> John 20:26–8

Maybe Thomas now realizes that Jesus is not just carrying the marks of the Roman nails but the scars of his own secret pain? Every pain, loss and sin Thomas had carried had been absorbed into the person of Jesus. Thomas doesn't need to reach for Jesus' hands and feet in this moment for he realizes that Jesus has unequivocally reached out to him. He doesn't need to touch the side of Jesus because he is experiencing Jesus' love and power touching the very centre of his being. He had thought he required a knowledge he could control to find peace of mind but now he is completely undone by a new form of knowing – an unfathomable and radical love. And this love is more than enough. Hope has been perfectly personified in the risen Christ. Thomas's response, 'My Lord and my God', is the heartfelt cry of a broken ordinary man realizing that nothing is too big for Jesus, no matter how big our pain, our loss or our doubts.

Meditating on Thomas's encounter with the resurrected Jesus inspired me to live my way into this resurrection life and taught me that nothing intimidates Jesus. There is no place he has never been, no grief he has never experienced, no pain he has never carried, no sin he has never paid for and no darkness he has never conquered! Everything matters to Jesus, nothing gets left out. He bore *all* our sins, carried *all* our sorrows, he absorbed them *all* into himself and through his resurrection it can *all* be redeemed. When revelation of what resurrection *really* means illuminates our beings, we, like Thomas, are left practically speechless. All we can mumble is, 'My Lord and my God'.

Thomas now knew that everything could be conquered by this resurrected Jesus with scars. This proved to be the inspiration for the rest of his days to LIVE THE RESURRECTION. He took the gospel to India and died a martyr's death.

Similarly, this is what my luminous darkness was all about. I needed to see for myself. Through an honest engagement with deep pain I became a candidate for deeper partnership with Christ. Through the midst of my heartache I had an opportunity to taste something of the new world breaking into the present. I have experienced new creation bursting into and through my mortal body. I didn't get all the answers, I haven't squared everything with a neat conclusion. Instead, I got him. I have resurrection blood pumping through my veins. He gave me himself, all of himself. He never invalidated my questions or squashed my protests, he simply eclipsed them with a revelation of his beauty, his awe, his strength, his intimacy. God's new-life-giving power has burst through the Sahara of my dead and dry heart like a pulsating, never-ceasing, overflowing spring!

ALL IS PRAYER

The final words of this book belong to the sacred words of the Psalms. The Psalms have accompanied us right through the luminous darkness of the grief tunnel. They have articulated the emotions of the pilgrimage. As we conclude this book with the theme of resurrection, it is fitting that the Psalms close with five chapters of praise.

Read these words slowly ...

> The LORD is gracious and compassionate,
>   slow to anger and rich in love.
> The LORD is good to all;
>   he has compassion on all he has made.
> All your works praise you, LORD;
>   your faithful people extol you.
> They tell of the glory of your kingdom
>   and speak of your might,
> so that all people may know of your mighty acts
>   and the glorious splendour of your kingdom.
> Your kingdom is an everlasting kingdom,
> and your dominion endures through all generations.

Psalm 145:8–13 NIV

Praise the LORD.
How good it is to sing praises to our God,

how pleasant and fitting to praise him!
The LORD builds up Jerusalem;
he gathers the exiles of Israel.
He heals the brokenhearted
and binds up their wounds.

Psalm 147:1–3 NIV

Praise the LORD.
Sing to the LORD a new song,
his praise in the assembly of his faithful people.
Let Israel rejoice in their Maker;
let the people of Zion be glad in their King.
Let them praise his name with dancing
and make music to him with tambourine and harp.
For the LORD takes delight in his people;
he crowns the humble with victory.
Let his faithful people rejoice in this honour
and sing for joy on their beds.

Psalm 149:1–5 NIV

Praise the LORD.
Praise God in his sanctuary;
praise him in his mighty heavens.
Praise him for his acts of power;
praise him for his surpassing greatness.
Praise him with the sounding of the trumpet,
praise him with the harp and lyre,
praise him with tambourine and dancing,
praise him with the strings and pipe,
praise him with the clash of cymbals,
praise him with resounding cymbals.
Let everything that has breath praise the LORD.
Praise the LORD.

Psalm 150 NIV

They are hymns of praise and adoration for Yahweh, the Maker and Sustainer of all! It all ends in praise. Rightly so! The story of the universe begins with God's glory and ends with God's glory. Isn't it beautiful that this undiluted praise only comes *after* the previous 144 Psalms, where the honest expression of every human emotion experienced in this life is described? Doesn't it reinforce the steadfast love, kindness, vulnerability, long-suffering and patience of a perfect heavenly Father that he would gift us with the full expression of every emotion of human life before we end it all in praise? Wasn't it clever of the Psalmist to construct the Psalms in such a way? Yes, there will be a crescendo of praise at the end of the Psalms, like there will be at the end of our lives, like there will be as we move out of our luminous darkness. But the praise will be all the sweeter, rounder and fuller when the full cacophony of the wounded and wonderful sounds of life have been expressed to the Maker of it all. For all of this, when surrendered to the Father, is worship. All of life is prayer. This is what the resurrected Jesus, 'Jesus of the scars', invites us into.

Therefore, I will hope in him alone.